thug

Thomas Kooler

thug

First Edition © Copyright August 2020

Worldwide Rights Reserved

The Americas Canada Mexico United Kingdom Denmark Finland Switzerland Northern Ireland Scotland Wales Sweden Austria Norway Germany Poland Italy Spain Portugal Greece Africa Australia New Zealand China Hong Kong Japan Singapore Philippines India Ukraine Soviet Union Gulf Nations Israel Ashland Grants Pass Coos Bay Pismo Beach Mars Jupiter Venus Pluto Moon

Author ~ Thomas Kooler
Editor-in-Chief, Steve William Laible, MBA
Contributor Mike McCune

Published by The Kodel Group, LLC
Imprint: Empire Holdings
P.O. Box 38, Grants Pass, Oregon, USA 97528
KodelEmpire.com

thug is meant only as percolating commentary on social injustice plaguing our down towns of our hometowns. This dialogue is of national importance, in both understanding the escalation of rhetoric and the deconstruction of our civilized society—namely, law and order. This unraveling of our democracy, our republic, must be addressed now more than ever. Social media and digital technologies have not only engaged but enlivened the disenfranchised by documenting grave injustices giving voice through captured imagery, hence memorializing extreme failures by law enforcement. The overriding concern now is how might we turn the corner and not only coexist but thrive. The concepts are solely of the author's imagination. The moral right of the author has been asserted. All Rights Reserved & protected under international copyright laws/conventions. Reproduction or distribution of this material via any means whatsoever, without the prior written consent of the author or publisher is illegal & punishable by law "except" in the case of brief quotations embodied in articles and reviews. Copyright © 2020 Thomas Kooler. Names, characters & incidents depicted are used by the author for illustrative purposes. Library of Congress Cataloging-in-Publication Data: Kooler, Thomas. Nonfiction. Social Sciences.

Library of Congress Control Number: 2020943002
Print ISBN-13: 978-1-62485-050-9
eBook ISBN-13: 978-1-62485-051-6

Printed in the United States of America, Europe, Asia, and beyond…

"Liberty cannot be preserved without a general knowledge among the people. Let us dare to read, think, speak and write."

~John Adams (1st VP & 2nd President)

"We advance, improve, evolve as a species/society only when more of us become engaged & enlightened through education-awareness-experience."

~ Steve William Laible (K-OR)

Americans are a responsible, loyal, and prideful lot. We are hard-working, kind and robust. Americans have the biggest hearts ever.

We are compassionate.

Watch us flourish in all manner of innovation, entrepreneurial endeavors, community volunteerism, philanthropy, social order and beyond once our citizens and perhaps more importantly, our government behaves responsibly, efficiently & honorably.

(Oh, and gets out of our way.)

~ Thomas Kooler

"America became the greatest nation on the planet because of a moral code; work ethic; heroes and people who knew what leadership and vision were."

The Kodel Party
[KodelParty.us]

Dedication

LeGend

***

Acknowledgments

Summary ~

When I saw the headline below in my local newspaper, it struck a nerve with me. This book is generated as a counterpoint to an editorial by syndicated  columnist Leonard Pitts, Jr. (Miami Herald) and the advancing tide of racism within our borders. His article has not been reprinted.

'Thug' becoming the new racial slur.

This work is a direct counterpoint opinion piece to his opinion piece.

Contributors: Mike McCune – History of the word 'Thug';

Cartoon by Andy Marlette (facebook.com/marlettecartoons) News Journal copyright creators.com 2014, posted on Mr. Pitts' public domain Twitter account.

Contributor
[Mike McCune]

thug

I was pleased to be asked by my publisher, Mr. Steve William Laible, to provide a contribution to the works of Thomas Kooler:

Personally, I rather enjoy discovering the origins of words that have been adopted into common usage; it's part of my stock and trade as a novelist.

As an example, I reference Leonard Pitts, Jr., syndicated columnist for the *Miami Herald* and his recent piece, *"Thug" becoming the new racial slur*. His slant comes from the November 2012 shooting in Jacksonville, Florida of a 17-year old Jordan Davis, a black youth, by Michael Dunn, a white man, and suggests the use of the word *thug* in our vernacular is replacing that of *nigger*.

However offensive, the two words have entirely different meanings.

Let's see what Miriam Webster has to say on the subject:

thug: n [Hindu & Urdu thag, lit. thief] [1810]: a brutal ruffian or assassin: gangster, tough – thuggery, *Thuggee*.

The Hindu root of thug, therefore, does not necessarily refer to a black person or to any other ethnicity, or to the type of loud music: 'thug music" (rap) that prompted the heated argument that resulted in the shooting of Jordan Davis. Given Miriam Webster's definition of *thug* as "a brutal ruffian or assassin," and taken with that context, would it not be correct to say Michael Dunn was the *thug*, and not the unarmed Jordan Davis?

Origin of the word: For 500 years (1336-1836) a secret and well-organized confederacy of professional assassins, called *Thuggee*, operated in India. Posing as traveling entertainers, thus insinuating themselves into confidence of encamped wayfarers and traders, they ritualistically strangled then plundered their sleeping victims, burying them in shallow graves or down the shafts of wells.

Though they traced their ancestry to seven Muslim tribes the Thugs, however, were **not** influenced by Islam but rather, worshipped Kali, the Hindu goddess of chaos and destruction. During their reign of terror it is said the Thugs were responsible for the murder of over two million people (some scholars suggest as many as three million).

Captain William Sleeman, an officer of the Crown's Dutch East India Company, finally infiltrated the Thugs. An expert at disguise, Sleeman spoke the Hindi dialects fluently, including Ramasi, the jargon of the Thugs that few outside their inner-circle understood. From 1831-1837, with agent Sleeman receiving cooperation from most of India's authorities, 3,266 Thugs were captured, of which 412 were hanged, 483 having given evidence against their confederates, the remainder being imprisoned for life.

If the word *thug* becomes so popularized by such incorrect usages as to be synonymous with the vulgar word nigger, it could warrant a second definition in Miriam Webster's dictionary. I doubt Webster would allow it. But really, Mr. Pitts, do we really need any more racial slurs than we already have as a means to hate one-another?

              mmm

Preface

Change begins with #R-E-S-P-E-C-T not violence!

- Otherwise, you suffer the unintended (yet wholly predictable) consequences.

#RacialDivide then continues. It's not a black/white thang as much as it is about taking responsibility for YOUR own actions: White AND Black, Asian AND Mexican AND...

If YOU are NOT part of the *SOLUTION* YOU ARE part of the *PROBLEM*. [So fix that.]

The rung of your personal enlightened ladder matters most!
- Character Matters!
- Integrity Matters!

A reasonable act of human kindness puts out a fire—doesn't start one.
- Defends a store, doesn't loot one.

An entitled, ignorant, arrogant mentality greatly and increasingly devolves a society.
- Looters, thugs & profiteers spit on the memories and souls of the deceased.

Evolve already...

Headlines

Realtor Group drops "*Master*" Bedroom.

Is it racist to produce only Caucasian [flesh colored] band-aids?

- ■ This author made a formal complaint with Johnson and Johnson over 25 years ago.

<u>Dateline</u>: June 2020 – Johnson and Johnson announce they are now in development to produce black and brown Band-aids. Subtle racism thwarted.

Who are the Johnsons? They were brothers **Robert**, **James** and **Edward Mead Johnson**, and in 1886, they brought together their respective talents to found a small family company that bore their surname. That company, of course, was Johnson & Johnson. When the trio launched their fledgling company, they had one building and just 14 employees.

Entrepreneurship. In 1954, at the encouragement of co-worker, a different, unrelated **Johnson** left the Fuller company and founded **Johnson** Products with his wife Joan, focusing on the **African American** male hair care market.

In 1971, **Johnson** Products became the first **African American-owned** company to be listed on the American Stock Exchange. Joan Johnson, who helped create one of the nation's largest black-owned companies, has died. Johnson, 89, co-founded Johnson Products Company, the pioneering black hair care company which made iconic products e.g., **Ultra Sheen & Afro Sheen**. She died Friday in Chicago after a long illness. She started Johnson Products Company in Chicago in 1954 with her husband, George Johnson.

They took a $250 investment and turned it into a multi-million dollar company which became the first black-owned company to be traded on the American Stock Exchange (now known as the New York Stock Exchange (NYSE).

"When I think about pioneers, the real pioneers are the people who are able to make a path where none exists," her son Eric G. Johnson. "Johnson Products in many ways was that company. She and my father had no provided path. They *created* a path where there was none."

~

Opportunities for minorities exist in "White" America. A preponderance of like-minded souls, rightly and more often wrongly, set the agenda, control the narrative, and own the day. Courage & Leadership are far rarer in politics because they play that game. Integrity is lost in the Congress, both sides, both houses. As the Majority Middle-Class, white and black, Mexican and Asian, Native Americans, we MUST rise up in one *collective* voice. Not with flaming torches but No. 2 pencils. That's how you truly effect change!! #VOTE

Ropes are nice when pulling down monuments but do you see the metaphor? Paint cans used to tag buildings or deface statues won't get your message across. We must instead use common sense. Put on our big boy pants & act responsibly like educated, reasonable, infused adults. First topic on the agenda is to make our mothers proud. Next, we must STOP anointing aristocrats, billionaires, bullies & bigots & especially conspiracy theorists as our Rulers. Only then can we truly address the devastating issues facing *"We the People."* You feel me?

~

There was once a time when a president was honored, police respected, newborns treasured and veterans revered. Let's strive to get there again…

How about tasers instead of deadly machismo-driven pistols or rifles slung over shoulders—as a taser says to me, "Hey, I'm only going to fuck you up in the moment, not steal your life."

Stand your ground. Speak your peace! Good soldiers follow orders. Great ones ignore unlawful ones!

Regardless, it is up to you to make better choices: Do not loot. Do not kill. Do not perpetuate racism. "Be the GOOD you want to see in the world." Tiny ripples.

Bold & Beautiful [Yellow Finger] *'in your face'* gesture by DC Mayor Bowser that White House is irrelevant, deaf & dumb. Who leads from the rear, as only cowards are known to do? Nations use diplomacy to seek resolution. Riots only exacerbate a situation.

They are the poor man's cry for change as they hold no legislative position or power. Riots actually alienate thereby creating a wider gap between races. Build bridges instead.

Responses
[Mr. Pitts' article]

Dear Mr. Kooler,

     I received your email. Thank you for writing. I or my assistant will try to get back to you as soon as possible. Please note that we do not open unsolicited attachments, and we do not read or respond to forwarded emails sent to mass-distribution lists, or to invitations sent via Twitter or LinkedIn.

Yours Truly,

Leonard Pitts, Jr.
Syndicated Columnist

Author of
"Freeman"
"Before I Forget" and
"Forward From This Moment"

-------- Original Message --------

Leonard Pitts Jr.
Syndicated columnist

Dear Mr. Pitts,

Re: A different perspective on your recent "Thug" opinion piece.

('Thug' becoming the new racial slur)

Enjoy and appreciate your column.
- ■ (Always well-articulated; thought provoking and rational.)

Did our mothers get it wrong: Stick and stones can break our bones…but words can never hurt you?

I took your word test and after closing my eyes, yes, a *California girl* conjured up a blonde, bikini clad, roller blading beauty; the *chess prodigy* word test was biased however based on my watching a recent segment on 60 Minutes on Magnus Carlsen. The grandmaster plays with his back to multiple players clearing the room with nothing but victories—ridiculously amazing at his gift, black or white.

Perhaps '*thug*' is a more politically correct word—for now. When I took you closed eyes word test, black males dominated my imagery. (Street corner/gangs/black criminals, and not educated, law abiding, professional black men.)

Perhaps also our mind's eye has been clouded with Crips and Bloods, the Civil Rights marches (for those who lived through the sixties, and more recently the Watts Riots, Rodney King and so on. If that is ALL anyone sees, why then of course, the mold has been set. Certainly if Hollywood embraced more people of color, we could in fact, form different opinions. Most Americans work and live within a thirty-mile radius. Most only glean what they see in the media. If it bleeds, it leads on the nightly national news. Black agitators are seen as good for nothing…because whatever it is they are agitated about doesn't likely involve Mr. & Mrs. White America.

So yes, there may indeed be a critical disconnect in our perceptions; yours too, based on each of our own experiences, witness, or otherwise draw conclusions from form those perceptions. As a national syndicated columnist, your readership is broad at best.

Here's the rub: The '*thug*' test results, for me at least, were flawed if not skewed from the moment you planted the proverbial mustard seed in my ear. Having first read your headline and article, I was doomed from the start—power of suggestion I suppse. So you must own some of what you profess inasmuch as you are at least partially responsible for perpetuating the coding of racial presumptions with your opinion piece.

I wouldn't expect you to think like a white man, nor I a black one. What's important is the ongoing dialogue of learned minds; youth and generational/geographical demographics. Hopefully we can all agree on some middle ground, agreeing perhaps, that yes, Rob Ford is a true Canadian national embarrassment; as was Jimmy Carter, George Bush (#43) in some circles, Bill Clinton in other circles, and a parade of Anthony Weiner's. From there we can push forward finding more answers, solutions, commonality. I say commonality, as this is the linchpin for acceptance or at least tolerance, as we continue defining our respective new normal(s).

However, I can prove your '*thug*' word test is flawed and NOT the new racial slur you hope it to be. I recently used the word 'Thug' for the FIRST time in my life, in a tweet. I have to admit, it felt good!

It was thoroughly descriptive, accurate and honest. The intent and connotation was spot on for this white boy. Thugs ought to be called out and held accountable; forcing the word 'thug' down our conscientious as a racial synonym (slur) is irresponsible—shame on Leonard Pitts Jr.

Do we really need to raise a new banner? Chastising users of the word, this word, severely misses the point. Those of you who are now championing this new touchstone *'thug'* to advance a racially biased lexicon is derogatory in itself.

An unfettered word becomes a racial inference only when cultural influences, slang or media hype it as such.

Meanings to words evolve organically, unless shoved down our collective throats. Assigning or associating words for races, agendas, or lifestyles dare I say, mascots, (brave, squaw, chiefs, redskins, renegade, pirate, Viking, black, gay, wetback, cracker, thug, etc.) is a very slippery slope indeed, worthy of an Olympic event; some of which warrant further discussions, if we ever hope to achieve enlightenment.

I'd like to present another perspective as to my 'intended' meaning of the word 'thug' as I used it. Please allow me to share a recent tweet of mine to a current U.S. Congressman and former Gulf War Marine, Undercover FBI Special Agent, the less than "honorable" Rep Michael Grimm (R-NY), who physically threatened to kill NY1 reporter Michael Scotto, after breaking him in half like a little boy, in an unbeknownst on-air tirade which captured the Congressman's shadow self.

Not the self we reveal when we know the cameras are rolling. A shadow self concealing the brute force bullying that is at the core of this disgraced representative's rant. He's only sorry he got caught. Isn't that always the case? The rant was a result of a perceived ambush question regarding the Congressman's federal investigation (campaign financing). <u>Neither the reporter nor the Congressman are black</u>. This is relevant to my initial point of your opinion piece: '<u>Thug becoming the new racial slur</u>. I disagree!

Another 'thug' is New Jersey Governor Chris Christy. He's a bully plain and simple. Power corrupts weak-minded souls. Their arrogance is dangerous. Whether he was behind #BridgeGate or not, the arrogant culture he fostered does not belong in government. Leadership is not that.

At any rate, thank you Leonard for pulling back the curtain on issues facing us as a society. tk

Subject: Re: Follow-up with 2 more thoughts from others....

RE: THUG
Opinion Piece
From: "Pitts, Leonard" <lpitts@miamiherald.com>
Date: Wed, February 19, 2014 11:26 am
To: info@kodelparty.us

Just an FYI, Mr. Pitts <u>never</u> writes his own headlines, and we don't even know what headlines a lot of other papers use. Each paper may write its own.

Judi Smith
Assistant to Leonard Pitts, Jr.

~

Hi, thank you. That's quite interesting and must be maddening at times.

I appreciate you sharing how these things work sometimes.

tk

-------- Original Message --------
Subject: RE: THUG Opinion Piece
From: <info@kodelparty.us>
Date: Mon, February 17, 2014 5:39 pm
To: "Pitts, Leonard" <lpitts@miamiherald.com>

Yes, thank you and I get that. [Perhaps being black is a sensitivity that warrants further thought?] Maybe, just maybe, those using "Chicago thug" for the president are simply calling him a BULLY!

But of course, that would be lost on you or anyone who is black. The natural conclusion is it MUST be a racist remark. That's sort of the problem, it's just too convenient for blacks to take everything as a racists' plot, when in fact, it is not always the case.

Perhaps he's just a bully from Chicago who just happens to be black. Can you see the leap you and others make? I am confident *'thug'* usage is veiled at times for the very meaning you suggest. However, rather than to buy into it, how 'bout we fight against assigning the meaning you infer? That's the article you should write.

I voted for Barack because of his incredible intelligence and articulation of his vision. Magnificent orator which seduces masses such as Dr. King or JFK or Lincoln did. They unite a nation, nay, the world. Our hope with Barack was of course dashed, or rather, quickly extinguished. His undoing was just too far-reaching in our conservative paced mind-sets. Visionaries are often misunderstood. (I ought to know.) ☺

He represented the peeps not elites.

This is a truly remarkable man. I don't blame him as much as I blame Congress for the state of affairs we find ourselves in today, namely Mitch McConnell, but that's getting much too far in the weeds.

Personally, I have only ever assigned 'bully' as the meaning of thug, but do realize others will likely do their own assigning; as you suggested.

Not that we will have any say on the matter, but perhaps we ought to fight harder against it be coined as a stereotypical 15 year old black child. The divide is wide enough. The last thing we need is yet another label. **Thug** deserves the proper meaning, that of **bully**! Which by all accounts is not a racist slur whatsoever?

Thanks again Leonard for your great columns.

Respectfully,

Thomas Kooler

P.S.

Leonard,

I asked another friend tonight, a 45 year old white female living in Sacramento, California and said, "what comes to mind when you hear 'thug'" she replied, "Bank robber." Perhaps a survey is called for eh?

Interesting huh? Seems us white folk aren't as racists as the other side would hope. Of course, living here in the Pacific Northwest we have a different perspective than say the south or eastern seaboard, Philly, Detroit, Chicago, Alabama, Louisiana, Georgia, etc.

I like this debate and I hope I can put to rest, or at least ease your mind, that while there is too much hatred and bigotry, and bullying, in classrooms, social media, professional sports, etc., no class, race or person should be lumped.

Maybe after hearing from more people you might likely have enough fodder for another less opinionated piece; one that balks at the assigned meaning. Try this:

"Thug, maybe NOT the racist slur I first thought" by Leonard Pitts Jr. (That would be honorable.)

I hope you are getting some great responses to your article.

Thomas Kooler

-------- Original Message --------

Subject: Re: THUG Opinion Piece
From: "Pitts, Leonard" <lpitts@miamiherald.com>
Date: Mon, February 17, 2014 12:52 pm
To: info@kodelparty.us

Apparently, I was not as clear as I should have been.

My point was not that "thug" means "black" at all times and in all situations, but, rather, that some of us are beginning to use it as a synonym for a certain racial slur. The clearest example of this is the insistence by many in the political right on referring to the president as a "Chicago thug."

Like him or loathe him, it is difficult to see where there is anything particularly "thuggish" about this often professorial man. It is impossible to understand their use of the term as anything but a racial code, in much the same sense that President Reagan once used "welfare queens" to disparage black women.
LP

Leonard,

Yes, that's EXACTLY why I pushed back. I wanted you to own (at least partly) when those in the media put out a headline as you did. "Thug becoming the new racial slur" is just so lopsided and biased in itself—it is RACIST! Learning later that you did not in fact assign the article's heading but rather those editors who carry your syndicated column did, makes this even more pervasive and problematic. Shame on those race-baiting editors at large—they must own it sharing in the racist tones they themselves perpetuate.

The following is what my 35 year brother in arms had to say when asked what 'thug' meant to him—without prodding. He is a white male, USAF, retired colonel, 56, who grew up in Alabama, educated in North Carolina now living in Tampa:

Thomas,

Yes, but he's still making an assumption on the "black thing." It never occurred to me that a "Chicago Thug", meant black, let alone the N word. If you had just said something about "Chicago Thug" without mentioning a person, I would probably have thought "mob" or gangster. Certainly not black. It really is the few that want to divide us that see meanings that maybe aren't there....

Johnny Southside
aka Tampa John
Life is Good!

Essay

thug

The information, guidance and suggestions in this handbook hopes to save lives. It's not at all provocative unless you consider a white man schooling black youth and their guardians as somehow crossing the proverbial line somehow.

It's meant to be helpful, insightful. If you have a problem with this book, then you are likely racist. Maybe it's subtle; maybe it's deliberate or pronounced. You ought not see color your own self as you judge the person behind this book.

You ought to only see the black ink spilled on a bed of white soiled cotton pages. There was that racist? Can a white person even say cotton anymore without being judged?

Or is it the way words are said? Wouldn't it be funny if after all is said and done, your stereotypes in place, I'z turns out to be just as black as you! Where will you be then?

This little exercise was meant to caution you on how words are used. Sometimes, they are just words. Maybe think of alternate possibilities of the intended meaning behind them.

thug the book was started in 2014 with a few email exchanges with a syndicated columnist and finished in the summer of 2020. [Lowercase thug is purposeful.]

thug puts forth a percolating commentary on social injustices plaguing our down towns of our hometowns. Chicago is a disgrace right now and has been for decades. There is zero *will* to truly correct the situation. Now, I want you to think about this: There are over 2,000 people shot in Chicago every year! Many hundreds die! This is not the America it once was. Most are black on black shooting with many more simply innocent bystanders. From children to seniors, senseless gang turf wars are chewing up this city and cities just like it, from Baltimore to Philly to Boston to Los Angeles. Talk about your repatriations.

Bringing slaves to America is wrought with both goodness and evil. More about repatriations later.

thug covers topics running rampant on our streets and in our homes such as domestic violence, bullying, school shootings, bad cops, racism, voter suppression, and repatriations while also offering some innovative solutions e.g., a new (Middle Class Party) movement that is ALL inclusive and better addresses these issues.

Neither Democratic nor Republican parties have truly addressed the multiple epidemics, let alone this current pandemic, coursing through our lives.

It is time for a majority middle class party. What we have now, simply cannot be the New Normal. We must search out innovative minds— those with no hidden agendas, those with real vision for **America the Beautiful**. (KodelParty.us)

This author also serves up some unsolicited advice on how your child might mitigate certain situations with the Popo and **Learn to Live!** Now, that's a banner I can get behind.

This continuing dialogue is of national importance—our very survival—as a civilized society, is in all our best interests save those agitators who would burn down our cities, do harm to our way of life. Those people must be banished from our shores. They do not want to be here. They do not belong here.

It's the only human trafficking that makes sense. We will work out a trade deal with other countries (Mexico, Russia, Ukraine, China, etc.) to accept our dissents. We however will not accept theirs unless they adopt the American way and assimilate. We must try different solutions. We must be innovative. Yes, some ideas will seem ludicrous, on the surface, but let's implement some pilot programs to gather hard evidence. Only empirical data will reveal if these tactics will create a more peaceful union.

"Together, with a little grace, we can make this world a better, kinder, safer place."

Steve William Laible (K-OR)
Kodel Party Founder

We will come to a better understanding when we halt the escalation of rhetoric and the deconstruction of our civilized society—namely, law and order. Law and order itself is suspect. It is being ignored, hijacked, or otherwise infiltrated.

    This is a time for reasonable minds to put our nation right. This unraveling of our democracy, our republic, must be addressed now more than ever. We have a lot of hate in this country because there is a lot of ignorance. At some point, we need to drop the hammer on good ole' white boys riding around in pickup trucks in otherwise peaceful neighborhoods, stalking their prey—an inquisitive young black man jogging through his own neighborhood who just happened to take a peek inside a construction site ought not be dead. Looking at construction sites is something I've done numerous times on my walks or jogs. It's interesting. Those three white murders need a jolt!

    Prison is too good for these murderers. I would instead take all three of these murderers to a tattoo parlor and cover every pore on their sickening bodies (with the exception of their palms and bottoms of their feet) with Nigerian deep dark ink! They will then walk amongst us for the rest of their days with a Scarlet letter.

Same for cops who shoot black men in the back, or sitting in their cars, or kneeling on their necks and throats, using chokeholds or otherwise carry out a cold blooded murder. That's dropping the hammer!

Social media's digital technologies have not only engaged but enlivened the disenfranchised as never before, by giving everyone a voice. We are witnessing more documented injustices by 'law enforcement' because of brave citizens giving voice through their captured imagery, hence memorializing extreme failures by law enforcement. Many are helpless, innocent victims who do not deserve to die. A stolen life actually terminates generations of potential future lives—those who might otherwise discover any number of things to advance and improve the human race.

Yet the lying sycophant, and ridiculous former New York City Mayor once stated on a Fox interview ... wait for it ... *"The truth is not the truth."* Can there be a more absurd human being? Why yes, yes there is but this is not a book about that. This aging decrepit former mayor does not speak for you does he? If so, then you are equally dressed in absurdity. And nothing written here will enlighten you. Underhanded people like this simply cannot be our political levers. They cheat. They stack the deck. They bait and switch. They above all else, LIE!

They lack such intense common sense we are all in peril. At this ignorance level our battle to right our majestic ship is a mighty task indeed. (Mixed metaphor for illustration only.)

The overriding concern now however is how might we turn the corner and do more than just coexist but rather thrive as a society rich with blessings, opportunities, kindness, education, goodwill and fabulous potential for a better quality of life?

Imagine what we could accomplish in all areas of endeavor if we could only stop bickering. Armchair quarterbacks are creating more discourse than solutions. Imagine this template of 531 Members of Congress.

Now try to imagine 531 chefs in one kitchen trying to plate a meal for a very special occasion with a few caveats such as a limited budget, hidden or self-serving agendas, a deadline, and so on. No wonder little gets done in the people's house. Now imagine, for sake of argument, we have 100M+ online warthogs pounding out their hate speech, trolling and trying to discredit those who hold different opinions or beliefs.

Pardon the pun, but it's a *recipe* for disaster. Nothing worthwhile ever comes of it. It's the same in Congress. The ebb and flow of bickering, compromise, deal making, hidden agendas, towing the party line without regard to truth, justice or common sense only creates a stalemate.

There is NO URGENCY in Congress!!

A stalemate has no winners or losers. Well, save the taxpayer who loses every damn time. We send too many Cyclops to Washington DC to address and structure real world solutions NOT for themselves personally but for the people they represent. Little gets accomplished because of all the saber rattling, jockeying for position, legal wrangling, and bills that ought to be no more than one page long. I don't care if it's a 17" ledger sheet of paper, no riders, no amendments, no pork barrel politics. Just pass the focused bill and write a new one for something else. Many a bill are weighted down with so much distraction they totally lose the point. This must stop.

Maybe we need a benevolent dictator.

It's a big ask, but it would help resolve or at least alleviate much of the insane brutality dividing our nation. First, we must all *avoid absolutes*. (You see what I did there?) I said we must ALL avoid ABSOLUTES. Sneaky huh?

We must no use all when judging cops or blacks or Mexicans, etc. You must learn to train yourself in mindful ways. You alone must shatter your preconceived notions.

Do not let the internet radicalize you.

Think for yourself. Even if you hear or read something that makes sense to you—all the more reason to investigate. Unlike the shady people of this word, endeavor to find truth where there is truth. In other words, you mustn't give in to #Stereotypical thinking. If we can 'ALL' at least start on the same page, there is hope.

But know this, "HOPE IS NOT A STRATEGY."
We hold these truths as self-evident:

1. Not all cops are bad!
2. Not all blacks are bad!
3. Not all Mexicans are bad!

Black culture alone has the power to help solve this problem with one behavioral modification. Unfortunately it has to come from black society.

Why?

Because it ain't coming from white cops in power. It ain't coming from their supervisors or the white court system. It ain't coming from politicians. Black culture must convey to their youth to zip it! Under no circumstance argue, fuss or fight with cops in the field! The streets are not the appropriate place to 'defend' oneself or make a case.

Don't try to explain your reasons.
- Don't resist commands.
- Yacky Yak, don't talk back.

Young men have a propensity to speak their minds. As do young black women but being thrown (hard) to the floor of your high school by an aggressive school resource officer is not a good outcome for voicing your hostile rants. No hissy fits or tantrums. (I was speaking to the men in the audience here.) Being taken to the hard, hot asphalt is not going to produce a good outcome.

Don't believe me. Go stand on your curb and just drop face first onto the asphalt. Now imagine doing that while being forced to the pavement. Not a healthy outcome—for you! Avoid body slams at all costs. Cops must NEVER operate this way. A body slam must be outlawed with severe consequences. There are better ways. Open your mind.

It's been my experience black people enjoy talking back. Whether with friends, teachers, police, authority or even movie screens in dark theaters! For some reason (enjoyment perhaps) they interject dialogue actually talking to the actors on screen—or warning them of some impending doom—especially if they are being scared out of their wits. It's a cultural thing I suppose.

Maybe they are wired this way or didn't learn common manners as a child. You never want to talk back to your mother, your grams or auntie, but especially cops. You never want to spit on them. The hammer will find you. Cops are people too. Show them respect and the good ones will treat you better. They certainly won't kill your children.

Now with that said, the hammer must come down on cops too. No cop must *hit* the streets without a psychological battery of tests. No cop should be allowed on patrol until they have say, two years under their belt shadowing experienced cops.

No Rookie with less than two years service will be allowed to carry a gun! No cops shall pull up on a scene based on a frantic 911 caller whining about a kid in a park with a gun without first assessing the situation.

Chicken shit rookie cops have arrived on scene and killed black children playing in the park with a bb or pellet gun. This should NEVER happen again. A child should NEVER be mowed down by a trigger happy motherfucking rookie cop. You can't be that dumb as to steal a life in the line of duty.

Think Beyond the Act

Police Commissioners, Sheriffs, 911 dispatchers, everyone, up and down the chain of command must be held accountable as well. A white woman who called 911 should not be murdered because a bad cop mistook her as a threat. She was only trying to get help and now she's dead.

Minneapolis: Justine Ruszczyk, 40 (white female) originally from Australia, called 911 on Saturday night to report a possible sexual assault in an alley near her home. Two police officers responded and one of them killed Ruszczyk. She died of a gunshot wound to the abdomen, an autopsy revealed. Officer Mohamed Noor, 33, originally from Somalia, has been identified as the officer who shot Justine Ruszczyk. He eventually received 12.5 years in a 3rd degree murder and manslaughter plea deal.

Cleveland: Nov 22, 2017 - No charges were brought after the 12-year-old **black boy** (Tamir Rice) was **killed** by a **ROOKIE COP** ... Rice was fatally **shot** by a Cleveland Police officer while playing in the **park**. ... the **toy gun** in question was an Airsoft **pellet gun**, which Rice got from a friend. But the 911 dispatcher never told officers that Rice was a **kid** or that the gun was likely fake. Or that Rice said his **name** and mumbled something about the **pellet gun**.

Ohio: Tyre King, a 13-year-old **black boy** is **shot dead** by a police officer in Ohio after allegedly drawing a non-lethal **BB gun** while being arrested. The **ROOKIE** officer who shot the boy was cleared of wrongdoing along with his partner. Officers responded to a report of an armed robbery of $10 in Columbus when they saw three male suspects matching descriptions given by the victim.

Two then ran off and were followed by police to an alley. Tyre King 'apparently' pulled out the gun and was shot multiple times by a **WHITE** officer.

Police later established the boy had actually been carrying a BB gun - a type of sporting air gun that is designed to shoot pellets - with an attached laser sight.

Parents, TIME for you to take responsibility in these acts of violence by cops on children because we cannot count on Rookie Cops to behave accordingly! They be undertrained and scared shitless with every encounter of a black youth.

So you have to step up and protect your children. DO NOT buy them or let them play with toy guns. The totally predictive consequence and sacrifices are just too great. Buy them a damn Barbie doll or Legos, Silly Putty, skateboard or something to keep them entertained—stop buying them or allowing them to play violent video games. Surely there is some responsibility with where we are today, due in some part to this multi-billion dollar industry affecting young adolescent minds.

It's HIGH time to retrain and fire bad 911 Dispatchers who put these preventable circumstances into motion. They MUST stop adding to the danger when some racist white person calls 911 complaining that she's being harassed or whatever by a perfectly legitimate black man taking his rightful place in that same park. Those who are terrified of black skin must be directed to Court Ordered desensitizing training for crying out loud.

NYC: White woman fired after calling 911 on a black man in Central Park. From Starbucks to the golf course to Dollar Stores to motel swimming pools, ignorant frightened WHITE people (men and women) are unnecessarily calling the cops on BLACK people.

STOP THE INSANITY!

911

911 Dispatchers, figure this out. Do your jobs. Racism is everywhere. But so are caviler attitudes—it's more than one bad apple—stop exacerbating the situation. You are indirectly responsible for killing children. Not ALL of you. You know who you are. It stops today! Fly a damn drone over the park. A child should not be shot within mere seconds of arriving on scene. That's a bad, inexperienced cop given bad information by a bad operator. Where do these people come from? Cities and departments need to do a better job hiring truly qualified people.

Call the ball.

I've known of drug addicts and dealers in my own neighborhood who drove our children to school in big yellow torpedoes. Alcoholics, criminals and alike should never be allowed behind the wheel transporting our children. I would bet every word on these pages, if you conducted a nationwide drug test on school bus drivers, for grass, Mary Jane, reefer, pot, weed, ganga, 420, dope, marijuana, at least 60% would test positive not that it's legal in many states. Don't believe, insist upon it. Test in every state.

We don't have a homeless problem, we have an drug problem in this nation. It's reached epidemic proportions. Our government has taken their eye off of the ball.

PoPo

POLICE

LAW ENFORCEMENT

The ONLY thing we must decide & implement in an innovative, civilized society and world power is how to deal with "bad behavior." Only **bad behavior**, not fear, race, gender, religion, or any other contributing factors must get in the way.

ONLY BAD BEHAVIOR endangers those of us who are otherwise law abiding and peaceful.

Whenever anyone endangers your life, it's normal to take issue with that. Road rage for instance, because you were cut off (likely by mistake) does not give you the right to release your inner, unbridled aggression. Pump the brakes. Take a beat—a breath. Think before you act. It's a discipline you must learn to implement. It's not unlike counting to 10. That act alone buys you some time to stave off your impulsive nature to act out. Don't escalate by making matters worse.

You must also be a full thinker. See it from the other person's point of view (POV). What would you do, react, seeing an enraged, aggressive person coming at you! You'd react. You'd defend yourself, same for them.

Drunken airline pilots, drug traffickers/addicts, speeding & dangerous drivers, texting or using your phone while driving, burglars, thieves, extortionist, morally bankrupt and criminally corrupt cannot and do not set the agenda.

Transients who endanger citizens and property, set fires, leave trash, needles, panhandle, commit crimes, defecate and fornicate in public places, and otherwise, threaten people, mock good order and discipline. They DO NOT set the agenda. We, as a civilized society must step up and take action. Civil Rights are all encompassing. We must fund and refocus our mental health systems with grace from the ground up. We must care for those who cannot care for themselves. That's leadership!

Where do we get the money? That's easy. The money comes from stopping our endless wars. A complete paradigm shift must occur. We must become the envy of the world. By ending wars and funding other regimes, we will invest in America the Beautiful instead. Sending trillions of America taxpayer dollars to other countries, dictators, foreign regimes, how we can ever truly improve upon our nation?

It's also time, once and for all, to stop putting good people in prison, but especially those who are not a threat to society. Besides, once incarcerated, the taxpayer foots the bill billions in construction and maintenance, medical and dental care, overhead, meals, wages and alike. We will never arrest or convict our way out of bad behavior. On the other hand, those who suffer from mental illness or make the life changing choices to commit crimes must be removed for an otherwise civilized society. By removed, I mean treatment centers not asylums.

I believe white people calling the Popo on blacks who are doing nothing more than occupying their space need more punishment than just being fired. They must receive mandated, court ordered boot camp of sorts—on a national scale. At least 30 days of intense immersion therapy. We must end this idiotic hysteria. If these people have mental health issues, those can also be addressed as stated above. During those 30 days of confined treatment, let white people touch black people's skin. Shake hands, hug even. Black people do not bite. (Well, that's no entirely true now is it?) For many, few older whites actually interact with other races. Youth, outside of hate groups are far more tolerate of mixing with or having personal relationships.

Oh I can see the folks in the south and Idaho grabbing their guns and taking a stand. Remember, these are only words. How you assign meaning to them is on you. Let them eat with them. Interact with theater, games, group sessions where they speak about what made them fear for their safety in the first place. Maybe if they learn more about the black culture, their roots, holidays, customs, history, children, pets, if they can lower their intolerances, even a smidgeon is a step in the right direction. Learned bigotry is a beast that must be slayed.

For those who flat out refuse to attend court ordered race relations treatment, levy a minimum ONE ((1)) year prison sentence on them! Period. Besides, it will do the nation a service to have these bigots off the street for awhile. It can be a special prison where there are ONLY black guards and staff. I'm just sayin'…

Fearing or hating blacks for being black is an unholy dimension of ignorance and it is a crime if they are denied service, harmed or discriminated in any way. It's a horrible imagination: Imagine being black and persecuted your entire life. Stop already.

In my hometown, there are maybe 4-6 black people. That's it. Imagine if the roles were reversed and you being white lived among say 50,000 blacks. Would you be comfortable or constantly on guard?

Now, speaking of BAD COPS, it is even more IMPORTANT to NEVER TALK BACK, SPIT, HIT or wrestle with a bad cop. No matter how wronged or confining, do not resist arrest. If placed in a police van without seatbelts, hang on for a bumpy ride. Protect yourself as best you can. The hammer will drop on those asshole cops soon enough. Make that report through your attorney once you are released. See, here's the difference, it's a distinction you won't be able to ascertain on your own, you aren't going to know which cops are good and which cops are bad.

It's not like they wear nametags or insignia or patches indicating as much. You must assume, for your own survival, that ALL COPS hold your life in their hands.

At this point, they are the authority lorded over you and you must not resist. This is not the time or place to misbehave. You must be disciplined. You must have patience. Speak only when spoken to.

Answer their questions politely, NEVER APOLOGIZE to them. "I'm sorry officer," should not be your default. It matters not. Hold your head high and proud. Own it.

By apologizing you are in essence admitting to wrong doing. Stop saying you are sorry. Save that for your family, the judge and jury should you wind up there eventually.

Be remorseful. Not for being black, not for being caught, but for committing a crime, if so charged. If you've done nothing wrong, then you have nothing to fear and certainly nothing to apologize for. Don't let your trial be played out in the street with some bad cop. Don't whine, don't plead, don't apologize. The streets should NOT be your trial by fire.

Just listen to their commands. You unknowingly intimidate them just by being black. To most bad white cops, you are a worthless *thug* to them, guilty until proven innocent. This is how and why they dehumanize you. It's not right, it's not fair. In street terms, you scare the shit out of them when you twitch.

Do Not Twitch! Definitely do not run. That is a primal instinct but so is chasing you down. It used to be a grave sin in the Wild West, worthy of hanging, when cowboys shot a man in the back. The difference today, cops do not see you as a man. Not even good cops. Otherwise, they would not protect bad cops. Peer pressure ought to force these bad cops from the rolls.

Do not move until directed or (commanded) to do so. This alone can save your life. Once a bullet leaves its chamber it cannot be retrieved until the Coroner removes it from your skull or body. The trick here is, to never give cops a reason to pull that trigger. Kids, never play with *toy* guns.

We must, no, you must, improve your odds of living. Toy guns are perceived as deadly weapons and rightly so. Things happen real fast in the field.

RIGHT TO LIFE

You protest, riot, demonstrate about how lives matter. Agreed. Every officer also has the right to protect his or her own life as well as their partners and the public at large. There is entirely too much disrespect for authority nowadays. Once that changes, change begins.

You will be amazed at how nice and polite cops are once they don't feel threatened and have the situation under control. If a cop axe for your license and registration, provide it. Do not speak until spoken to. Think Military Boot Camp Recruit. If you are participating in criminal behavior or activity at the time, all the more reason to keep your mouth shut—other than to axe for an attorney. Do not however be too eager.

Wait until you are Mirandized (read your rights).

To wit: *"You have the RIGHT to remain silent. Anything you say can and will be used against you. If you cannot afford an attorney one will be provided for you. Do you understand these rights?"*

You do not want to be axing for a lawyer before being placed under arrest. [Note: *axe* was being used to better relate with you and see if you're paying attention.] It was NOT a racists act or inference. And let's be real, you know its *axe*!

Think back to those incidents you've seen on television or the internet. Most confrontations escalate when black men or black women start arguing with cops. Being in the field is NOT the appropriate place to test your case. Maybe black people did not enjoy the benefit of my mother and manners who taught me not to talk back at the age of 5! It's our culture you really might want to adapt. I know your momma taught you better. So basic.

The problem we are seeing now (disrespect for authority) comes from an entitled generation who honestly believe it is their God given right to mouth off. Trust me, not the time or the place. Save it for the courthouse. #Conform #Comply Give the #Respect you seek. And don't be an ass. The cop is NOT your yes, Master. Don't even go there. Respect the uniform if not the man. Respect the badge if not the man. Respect yourself!!!

Whether two cops or six, cops will always win in a takedown! Cops are highly skilled, hyper vigilant creatures on the hunt for criminals. EVERYONE they stop is presumed to be a criminal unless or until they do their field investigation.

They rely on their training, their experiences, your answers to their questions, mannerisms, and more to evaluate and determine who they have stopped. Yes, even those who have fallen asleep in their cars, parked in a Wendy's drive-thru. Had that *gentleman* (Rayshard Brooks of Atlanta) not run like a scared, drunken fool rabbit, but rather allowed the officers to handcuff him, he would be alive today. Again, running from a wild beast will end with the same result of you being dead.

DO NOT RUN FROM COPS.
(Bears repeating!)

I promise you, if you give respect, any Crip, Blood, MS 13 gang member, prison inmate or prison guard or military enlisted or officer will tell you this:

R-E-S-P-E-C-T
MATTERS!

Please understand this. Respect cops but also RESPECT yourself. Cops have earned and deserve your respect. Well, at least their uniforms and badges have earned your respect. That's really the integral key to success here. It will be returned. Think of RESPECT as street currency. Everyone wants it! Every cop stop doesn't have to be a hostile event.

It doesn't have to escalate. You don't have to die. Take responsibility for escalating the matter yourself. Do what you can to defuse the situation.

If you are an African American or as I like to say, American, taking issue with this book or the author "a privileged white guy" telling you how to behave, then you're missing the point or *you* might be the racist as previously stated. Keep an open mind. TRY to learn something here.

Handbook for Life

Okay, please don't misunderstand the intentions of this ***Handbook for Life***. It's meant for you to live. 'Handbook to Live' might be a better title. It's NOT my job as an author to school you or law enforcement on how to behave. That was your mammas' job or auntie, grandparent or guardian.

My goal here is to give **you** the information that can actually save your life. I'm just a Cracker Man who believes in fixing things. (Or am I just pretending to be white?) Truth be told, I'm not the kind of guy who fixes things. I'm the kind of guy who pays others to fix things. The point is, in this case, I believe I can help, for those willing to listen. Too many black men, women and children are being murdered in cold blood by law enforcement and gangs.

It stops now!

Cops have indeed lost sight of *their* true objective—to apprehend. Detectives investigate but beat cops are paid by taxpayers to assess, de-escalate, apprehend (arrest). Maybe traffic cops should stay in their own lane. Cops somehow, got it in their heads it was also in their job descriptions to apply a little street justice, a tune-up, if you will. These cops must be deleted from the registry if they cannot be retrained to better respect their position, uniform, badge, and YOU.

"You can judge the size of a man by the size of the things that bother him."

Apply that to your own life. Live by it. The system must change and be more responsive to the horrific injustices plaguing OUR black youth, men and women in this country. That said the #BlueLine must never close ranks on injustice. To do so is cowardly. It lacks integrity. Be Better!

When a bad cop, and this includes racist cops, who behave badly:

-- Justice must be swift, firm and fair and not delayed or swept under the rug or ignored. *Arrest bad cops on the spot!*

-- A different kind of movement is necessary.

-- It needs to come from #WhiteSociety

-- The #PoPo must be repurposed.

- ■ Defunding Police Departments is asinine, ludicrous.

SWAT teams exist for extreme situations. We need to implement a new paradigm for policing. One that is responsive to the good order and discipline of themselves and the public. Traffic cops have been empowered to murder people. This must end now. Rookies must never be alone in the field and they are never allowed to carry a gun or live ammunition.

First and foremost, STOP COMMITING CRIMES. Then we can put cops in their retirement homes. Secondly, since no race is going to stop their bad behavior, there must be another answer. Did you know between Alexa & Google, there 36,000 cops in New York City alone!

There are 800,000+ sworn police officers in the United States. Add another 35,000 FBI agents, 3,000 Sheriffs (not including the cadre of Barney Fife deputies), add another 4,000 Marshals and Deputy Marshals, and lastly, 166 Texas Rangers.

Maybe if people weren't committing crimes, we wouldn't need so many police officers. Ever think of that? Maybe it's human nature to rob, steal, cut, shoot, kill, swindle, speed, drive drunk or impaired, rape, etc. Maybe, just maybe, those sworn to uphold laws are either growing numb to it all or completely burnt out and frustrated and therefore taking it out on everyone, even or especially on innocent black suspects.

The best answer is probably somewhere between those lines. No matter. Walk a mile in law enforcements boots and see what they see. Your opinions and level of understanding will improve. Imagine a job where every single day someone is trying to KILL YOU! If you don't think this puts stress on police officers you would be wrong. Catching bad guys is a rush for them. That's a stress reliever—in the moment.

Peace Officers + Non-Peaceful People = 2,300,000 (2.3M+) people incarcerated (in prison) in the USA! And yes, of course, not everyone in prison is guilty, even though they were found *guilty* by a jury of their *peers*. But wait, that's an entirely new subject and a different debate worth having. [A discussion to follow a little further in this essay.]

What's wrong with the human condition?

Number of Police Officers: Chicago (10k), Los Angeles (10k), Boston (2K), Tampa (1k), Atlanta (3k), Dallas (7k), Kansas City (2k), Baltimore (3k), Raleigh (3k), Jacksonville (4k), Washington DC (4k), Minneapolis (3k), New Orleans (2k), Las Vegas (3k), Tulsa (2k), Alaska (3k), Portland, Oregon (3k), Albuquerque (3k), Wilmington DE (3k) Miami (2k), Houston (10k), Phoenix (8k), Milwaukee (3k), Philadelphia (9k), San Antonio (8k), San Diego (7k), San Jose (5k), San Francisco (5k), Denver (3k), El Paso (3k), the entire state of Rhode Island (5k), South Carolina (24k), South Dakota (4k), Maine (6k), Idaho (8k), Vermont (3k), Wyoming (2k)…Let that sink in for a moment.

Do the arithmetic! What costs to taxpayers do these salaries, court costs, imprisonments add up to? Why do 'we' as humans behave so badly? Why are criminal acts in such large quantities that it requires 36,000 men and women police officers in one city? Wouldn't you want to live in a world where we didn't need police officers because 'we' never (or rarely) committed crimes?

Maybe

Maybe being a *'nation of laws'* has doomed us. Maybe there ought to only be 4-5 laws and that's it. Okay, maybe 9 or 10. #Commandments ~ Surely we can write an algorithm that serves us all with respect to law and order, good order and discipline. It really just boils down to common sense—treating yourself and others with respect. The differences between right and wrong aren't that difficult to distinguish.

We've overcomplicated it. They system is broken. Maybe we allow sex workers to earn a decent living, which might end (or reduce) rapes and human trafficking. Don't be mislead into believing that 'rape' in ONLY about power and control. Remember to steer clear of 'absolutes.'

Rape is *also* about SEX! Maybe the BEST way to protect women is defuse men's' carnal knowledge.

Those who rape children (priests) must be exiled to an island or another country. Dip them in purple so the world can know their sins. Maybe we decriminalize drug use but not manufacturing or distribution or maybe we work to improve young lives so they never even attempt drugs in the first place. It really is about peer pressure, experiment, and reckless behavior. There we go again; bad behavior seems to be the common denominator!

Maybe we need to look at traffic stops differently. Maybe cops aren't armed. Maybe funding a city or state can come from other revenue sources. Maybe a series of checkpoints is needed much like truck stops. Chasing vehicles is problematic. Maybe a massive helicopter (Mil Mi 26) can drop in with a massive net instead of spike strips or claws and just lift those fleeing cars on the I-10 freeway and drop them out to sea.

Anyone driving under the influence needs to lose their vehicle. Confiscation of a deadly weapon is mandated for first time offenses, period. That's a true & immediate consequence. There are drivers who have dozens of DUIs and yet they still drive. Vehicles can then be resold on the open market with proceeds going toward law enforcements, victims, education, treatment, etc., or returned to the lien holder. Maybe we can *fine* our way out of specific offenses and not tie up the courts.

Are we just lazy by nature looking for a quick buck? Are 'we' so smart, 'we' can steal from unsuspecting or vulnerable citizens? Must we kill everyone who disagrees with us? Why kill the husband or cheating wife? Just divorce them and move on. Are we that emotionally unstable we can't handle a little bedroom disappointment?

Maybe you get a $10k or $25k windfall in the divorce because of a cheating spouse and their companion—payable as an annuity over time by both cheating parties to their significant spouses—and no fair trying to entice your spouse to cheat just so you can earn a payday.

Maybe, instead of killing a cheating spouse, the system rewards you (the victim of a broken heart) with $25k as compensation, pain and suffering. (These award judgments can be scaled.)

It preserves your freedom while enriching you. That's a pretty good incentive.

Maybe we pay bank robbers not to rob banks, you know, for good behavior. Sound crazy? We have to look cray-cray to find solutions wherever they hide.

"If we always do as we've always done, we'll always get what we've always got."

Look, if loans were made less complicated with lower rates, maybe desperation is reduced. Look, it's a game when criminals try to steal cash from an armored truck, bank, jewelry store, homes, and businesses, embezzlements. Banks also steal, legally, credit cards is how. 29+% (usury) is a crime! Many rates charged by PayDay loan companies can reach 500%!!

u·su·ry
/ˈyoōZH(ə)rē/

noun
the **illegal action or practice** of **lending money** at **unreasonably high rates** of interest.

Yet banks get away with it. If rates were lower, fewer people would default thereby mitigating financial institution's losses. It's systematic racism and Highway Robbery when a $2k credit card balance takes 30 years to pay off when making only minimum payments.

When it comes to your financial health, minimum payments on your credit cards are poison. A $2,000 credit balance with an 18% annual rate, with a minimum payment of 2% of the balance, or $10, whichever is greater, would take 370 months or just over **30 years** to pay off.

Is this a **racist tactic by banks** to keep black and brown families down!? Think about that.

398%
Payday Loans Are Very Expensive – High interest bank credit cards might charge borrowers an APR of 28 to 36%, but the average payday loan's APR is commonly **398%**. Payday Loans Are **Financial Quicksand** – Many borrowers are unable to repay the loan in the typical two-week repayment period.

How about you stop giving your hard-earned money to these institutions? How about Congress take this issue by the balls and fix it instead of jockeying all day long who has the bigger ...

The Middle Class NEEDS-REQUIRES-DEMANDS better and truer representation at all levels of government but especially in Washington DC.

KodelParty.us

For instance, their platform is to END ALL TAXES as we know it and repurpose the IRS. A Kodel Party Administration will create a new revenue stream that benefits the hard-working middle class once and for all.

It allows you to keep your entire paycheck! Not one deduction, not even for state and federal withholding, health care or Social Security. Your standard of living is improved immediately by taking home more cash every single week.

If a rich uncle or auntie leaves you an inheritance that too goes to you without taxation. Gone are sales taxes, income taxes, property taxes, capital gain taxes, state taxes and those pesky surcharges found on everything from telephones to tires and gasoline. The entire lot of taxes and all that goes with it, such as annual filings, tax dodging, deductions, all go away. The billion dollar companies and wealthy never again dodge paying their fair share, or any share for that matter.

Imagine how your quality of live will improve once you no longer have to pay property taxes for example. For those owning or buying their homes, that's hundreds of extra dollars in your pockets!

The power shifts back to the consumer. Wall Street and our 50 States fund the US Treasury directly, not individuals.

As a country, we waste so much money. That ends. No longer will US taxpayers fund or prop up foreign regimes. We send trillions of dollars annually to other countries. Imagine what our programs, medical care, infrastructure, our down towns of our hometowns would be today had we invested those trillions upon trillions of our own money on America the Beautiful instead!

KodelParty.us

Truer Middle Class Representation for America the Beautiful.

The 800lb Gorilla in the Room!

If you see this as a racist heading, adjust your thinking. It's a 'common' term. It simply means something with a large presence that doesn't get talked about. Or can do anything it wants because it's so powerful. A person or organization so powerful it can act without regard to the rights of others or the law. And that's precisely what we're discussing here. Yes, I realize I could have used an 800lb elephant—author prerogative.

800,000+ cops in the USA! That must tell you something. Maybe, just maybe these riots, protests, demonstrations are looking in the wrong direction. How about a little torch lighting on a much bigger problem plaguing our nation—Bad Behavior. There are a lot of bad guys (criminals) out there. Something has to give. But here's the deal, not all bad guys are the same. Not all cops are the same.

It is not about victim blaming or shaming. The caveat being, having, showing, demonstrating R-E-S-P-E-C-T for #Authority! This is where we fall short. I come to this conclusion based on my 22 year distinguished military career beginning at 18 years old. I learned to follow orders. Do "exactly" what I was told. Respect for authority not because they were right necessarily, but because they had power over my livelihood. I listened. I complied. It is a learned disciplined.

Fewer of our youth are learning the valuable lessons they should have learned at home. Family values are in steep decline. Many young adults believe *'entitlement'* is a right when that's simply not the case. Many are being wised up with street smarts and nothing will ever change if we keep doing the same things.

We must pivot as a nation.

PEERS

While we're at it, paradigm shifts being what they are, the judicial system needs an overhaul as well. A jury of your peers ought to mean, people who are *equal* to the defendant in abilities, qualifications, age, background, and social status. How 'bout we add *ethnicity* as a top peer priority in jury trials. I highly doubt a black man standing trial in the South with a jury of his non-peers [white men and women] every stood a reasonable chance—hence wrongly convicted because they only saw his black skin or convicted on stereotyping. Certainly an algorithm can be written to include a far better and fairer jury pool. Why do you suppose innocents are in prison?

As we all know, in the movies, those wearing the black cowboy hats are the villains and the white cowboy hats represent good. It's the classic good versus evil doctrine. Dark verses White.

What a horrible societal disgrace to be viewed as guilty just for being black. Hollywood has perpetuated this underlying racist stereotype for generations. Of course, there will still be some obvious biases and guilty black men will go free as all black juries would understandably overcorrect. Trust the system but only when it is blind to color. A gay defendant's jury must ONLY consist of gay jurors. Make sense?

Maybe ONLY black cops can arrest black suspects. Maybe it should be illegal for white cops to stop, question or arrest outside of their own race.

"A Jury of Your Peers!"
[Literally defined as equal justice under the law.]

In sociology, a peer group is both a social group and a primary group of people who have *similar* interests, age, background, or social status. The members of this group are likely to influence the person's beliefs and behavior. Peer groups contain hierarchies and distinct patterns of behavior.

Sitting a jury of patriotic warm bodies and those who would rather be anywhere else, is not a peer group. Let's address and correct this, okay?

Author's Perspective on Authority

As I grew older (and yes, wiser) I definitely pushed back on authority whenever I felt the order or circumstance was wrong. As I rose in the ranks from an enlisted airman to a captain, I grew bolder, more confident and assertive with injustices. No longer an airman, now a commander of troops, I had some sway and influence and pushed back within the system. The operative word here being *'within'* the system.

The pen is mightier than the sword.

I also gained some perspective as the president of a parole board. Trust me when I share this, the military services has a full complement of bad behavior, from indecent exposure to murder; from rape to larceny. Torching my Base Exchange (BX) or Commissary would have landed me in Leavenworth Penitentiary. I did not topple statutes. I did not set fires or loot my Air Force bases. I did not destroy neighborhoods or down towns of hometowns. I did not riot or loot to make changes within the system. I took a more reasoned approach to effect change. That's how the white man rolls.

What's occurring in our cities across America now is sickening, ignorant and wholly uncalled for. Mob mentality is never the answer. It only destroys.

The Insurrection Act of 1807 is a United States federal law that empowers the president of the United States to deploy U.S. military & federalized National Guard troops within the United States in certain circumstances, such as to suppress civil disorder, insurrection and rebellion.

Let's be clear, protesting in the name of #Floyd is NOT an #Insurrection ~ Nobody is trying to overthrow the government! It is instead about racist cops killing black men & women, point blank. It is instead about applied justice in unequal measures. It is about change not toppling a regime. It is about warranted civil disorder & rebellion meant to bring about accountability for those sworn to Protect & Serve. Tuning up blacks #StreetJustice is not the job of cops.

Apprehension ought not be a Death Sentence.

If you think American Armed Forces have the stomach to Thrust Advance Thrust slaughtering innocent American Protesters with their Bayonets then we have slid down that proverbial slippery slope and there is no coming back from that.

America the Beautiful requires a preponderance of like-minded citizens who can quickly identify Right from intolerable Wrongs!

A preponderance of like-minded souls, rightly and more often wrongly, set the agenda, control the narrative and own the day. Courage & Leadership are far rarer in politics than any profession on earth. As the Majority Middle-Class, we MUST rise up in one collective voice. We MUST stop anointing aristocrats, billionaires, bullies & bigots & especially conspiracy theorists as our Rulers. Or not...

Racism is deeply rooted in learned behavior, insecurities, morals, prejudices, hatreds. This are manifested in dwindling populace but rears its ugly head whenever and wherever leaderships gives permission to be ugly and destructive.

You gotta train your mind to be stronger than your emotions or else you'll lose yourself every time. [Shortquotesworld.com]

CIVIL UNREST

Life on this planet is short. We either decide we want to live with war, hate, crime and tragedies, or in the lap of luxury in the greatest nation on earth. Luxury meaning the freedom to pursue life, liberty and happiness.

Tremors of civil unrest are percolating. Our national fabric is fractured. Immigration, homelessness, crime, mental illness, child & spousal abuse is increasing beyond our control. We are devolving from a civilized society. Perhaps and in part, because lack of funding, or in the prioritizing of funding or providing opportunities, education. Hopelessness is more prevalent now than ever.

Homelessness is numbering in the tens of thousands. These aren't just addicts, hobos or drunks anymore. These are moms and dads and children. Families are living in their cars, shelters, on streets, & under bridges. When did a home for middle American start pricing out at $400,000?

It's time to fix this horrendous situation, once and for all. It can happen to you. We are not the U.S.S.R. or North Korea. It's funny what one "learns" to accept...if it happens gradually enough. The Kodel Party says, enough is enough! It's time for a new American Agenda!

The Kodel Party endeavors to revamp the entire incarceration system from the ground up. The first premise is, there are BAD people in this world. There are also good people who exhibit BAD BEHAVIOR. There is a distinction to be made.

A system is broken beyond repair for anyone to have a rap sheet. Dozens of crimes or scores of pages listing hundreds of crimes simply means this person simply cannot conform to laws, a civilized society, and is making a choice to hurt people and themselves. Make no mistake, it is a 'choice' to be broken. No one is born under a dark cloud. Every decision has a consequence, period.

We mustn't look at incarceration as an income stream. No "for profit' institutions will exist under a Kodel Administration. Only violent criminals will be housed. That 'housing' WILL NOT be within our 'society' but outside of it

kodelparty.us

Taken from the KodelParty.us website

It's also time, once and or all, to stop putting good people in prison or those who really aren't a threat to society. We will never arrest our way out of this bad behavior. On the other hand, those who suffer from mental illness or make the life changing choices to commit crimes must be removed from a civilized society.

This must be done as humanely as possible. It's not about locking people up and throwing away the key. Mental illness/wellness care treatments and management of these destabilizing and debilitating diseases must become a thriving priority in our society. As a loving and compassionate nation, we must care for our broken souls. It's really that simple.

Good cops are great!

-- Bad cops must be weeded out and reallocated to a better vocation.

(Prison being one option.)

The stresses of their jobs, however, should leave no one sitting in judgment. Until you are spit upon, punched, disrespected, shot or otherwise infuriated by those individuals who would not be welcomed at your dinner table, let's begin to look at these men and women in uniform as the true American heroes they are.

Granted, law enforcement has some thinking they are judge, jury and sadly executioner. The street justice and tune-ups must stop. We must provide better training of our officers. Their job descriptions must be reinforced and dealt with before another life is lost.

I personally believe it boils down to R-E-S-P-E-C-T. Maybe not a simple solution but it's a step in the right direction. Even gangs know this. Respect must go both ways! Cops are NOT better than those they stop & question. Their sole job is to protect and serve. To resolve, defuse, deescalate, assess ... wait for it ... apprehend!

There is NEVER a valid reason for shooting & killing a man in the back who is fleeing.

Maybe cops need to hook boxing gloves (without thumbs) call them leather mittens if you will, to their utility belts. This will prevent an overt action by the 'suspect' grabbing and firing a gun. Or perhaps a net to shroud & tangle the 'suspect' especially those 14 year old girls who are slammed to the ground in a ill-conceived, macho take-down in a classroom or pavement as we've all seen on television. These actions must NEVER be condoned! But prosecuted.

It's ridiculous for anyone being questioned by police to start arguing or debating their point or challenging officers to a wrestling match. A take-down can and does have deadly results of innocent "dead right" victims. Maybe it's a cultural thing. Talking back to a theater screen is funny but talking back to authority is disrespectful & unwise. Knock it off. Show these men and women in blue the respect they deserve. Stop arguing or evading or otherwise putting yourself in peril. Go with the nice policeman and sort it out later.

Is your grocery store clerk ready to step in front of a bullet for you? How about your accountant; banker; paperboy; mayor; trash collector; gas station attendant; doctor, dentist, house painter, plumber, veteran, etc.

The answer is yes, many would on instinct or impulse. But not on a daily, thoughtful basis. Every day a cop dons that uniform and even in plain clothes, they pledge their lives for total strangers as part of their job description.

<u>We must fight against stereotyping or stereotypical behaviors or attitudes.</u>

Not all cops are bad. Not all African-Americans are bad. Not all Muslims are bad. Not all Mexicans are bad. Not all White people are bad. Do you understand this?

TRAINING

Innovate Equip Train

The answer is NOT to defund our police departments but to retrain them with an emphasis on honor, duty, service. Then hold them accountable by erasing the blue line they hide behind. Never again will they be held above the law.

We must continue to innovate, equip, train and reward our protective forces as they put their lives on the line every single hour of every single shift.

Think what that means for a moment. Men and women are willing to die for you!

That's pretty incredible. Their loyalty, patriotism and duty shall be admired and rewarded.

Hopefully and eventually, we can eliminate every law enforcement position on the planet. That is, once all the bad guys & dolls have been caught, given up or been reallocated to a space outside of our 'civilized' society.
Until then, we will help our law enforcement professionals close the gap on crime by listening to them and enacting laws that help them do their jobs better, safer, kinder. And the issue isn't about banning weapons from citizens. However, we can set in place incredibly important legislation with respect to firearms & responsibilities for each owner.
(Note: those are not the bad guys.)

The consequences of using a weapon in the commission of a crime, is the general premise of our philosophy. Consequences of actions carry the weight, not the mere possession of...a gun!

The Kodel Party will put forth an Amendment that removes rights for citizens known to be a habitual detriment to society, law and order. We need a carrot and a stick to make this work. A provisional circumstance may restore said rights once rehabilitation and restitution are accomplished.

While our military forces are now held in the highest regard, with the gratitude of a grateful and free nation, so shall our domestic heroes. Until the day we no longer need police forces, or intelligence agencies, etc., we will support them with the highest priority this nation can offer.

Governors will undoubtedly show likewise support for their entire civil service legions of administrators and those who have sworn oaths to protect and serve.

Chicago wants us to believe that Black Lives Matter. Why then do they lead the nation in gun violence? Over 90 shooting deaths in ONE weekend alone with nearly 500 victims in same ONE weekend! That's a crisis! And deserves our attention and ACTION! Of course black lives matter so who is this directed at? The police? Whites? That's pretty misguided. How about this:

A national call to order that ALL LIVES MATTER. Stop with the divisive segregation and attack the nut of it.

Humankind must stop killing one another and continue evolving using good sense & common sense not brooding hostilities, territorial turf, drug or gang wars to resolve disputes or paybacks.

Education, enlightenment, ethics, opportunities must replace violence in our streets. We advance, improve, evolve as a species/society ONLY when more of us become engaged & enlightened through education-awareness-experience.

A gun is no more responsible for killing than a pencil is for misspelling a word!

A simple act of caring creates an endless ripple.

Baltimore you are being stereotyped. When a nation watches civil unrest in your city of course the logical conclusion is to paint every citizen as a punk. Be more productive! Show leadership! Mob mentality, Destruction, Social Disobedience has lasting, unintended, deadly, consequences.

EVOLVE! Our children are watching. Looters, thugs & profiteers spit on the souls of the deceased and every child of color with your bad behavior! Redirect your frustration!

We once had black airmen take over a mess hall in the seventies. It needed to be handled with respect not brutal force. The TOP SECRET answer here to resolving most problems, disputes or disagreements is to ... wait for it ... LISTEN!

As a Commander, I could not fix a problem that I did not know existed. It's important to elevate your concerns within the system to those who are the shot callers.

(Wait, bad terminology.) Elevate your concerns to those who have the authority and means to make decisions. As the Executive Officer for three base Commanders, I learned how to resolve issues by listening, mediation and compromise.

I once had to confront a base housing resident who decorated his home for Halloween with a mock lynching! Fully dressed dummies swinging by the neck, rope tied to a tree branch in the front lawn visible to everyone! This was at a former high-desert California Air Force Base, now closed.

The neat thing about being in the military is you don't have to ask. You can order (boss) people around. It's so fun. I didn't have to have a discussion about why this might be highly inappropriate or seen as insensitive, even as a Halloween yard decoration. Murder scenes and decapitations were okay though. Go figure.

The sergeant would dare not talk back to a commander. Officers lord power over enlisted knowing full well, our word is final. There is no debate. No screaming at me, or spiting in my face or arguing with me. The civilian populace would be so much better off if they adopted basic rules of civility with police. What right do you have to argue or spit on or otherwise treat an officer of the law with such great disrespect?

I didn't have to listen to his reasons. I ordered that crap be taken down immediately. I ought to have tossed the Sergeant in the brig. A definite court-martial or non-judicial punishment (Article 15) was called for, where we can dock their pay or demote them, but the Commanders over me, let it drop. Was it bad behavior, racism or simply poor holiday judgment?

During Desert Storm, as the Group Mobility officer for an F-4 Wild Weasel fighter wing, it was my job to marshal base personnel (800+) and cargo to the flight line so Load Masters could secure airlifts and ready deployments.

We were about to engage with the 4th largest army in the world—and Saddam's elite Republican Guard. One particular push back I championed was when headquarters Tactical Air Command (TAC) sent a direct order that no Air Force personnel would be permitted to carry a Bible or anything religious into country.

That did not set well with me. Our political 'leaders' said it would 'offend' the Kuwaiti and Saudi governments with whom we were defending from Saddam's invasion. Oh boo who. We were about to spill our blood yet again on foreign soil fighting another countries war and they denied our books of faith. I don't think so! Not on my watch. Attica. Attica. Attica.

I was at my 20th year in the military and my retirement was secured. I launched a campaign fighting against HQ that this order would NOT be followed or carried out.

You see, politics had come between warring nations and the US was asked for help in stopping the invasion. Our personnel were putting their lives on the line—not for our country but the Middle East. To deny faith in the military was a non-starter. I instructed everyone to belay (ignore) that order, that directive. Never again shall Congress put that burden upon our troops.

At any rate, I was within mere hours of takeoff, my bags packed for a long deployment, when commanders above me, pulled me from the mission. Likely anticipating I would land in country as the A-Team leader and take the fight to Muslim countries myself for all the human rights violations they place on their subjects—being a kingdom and all. They could not afford an international incident I suppose.

I was not deployed (Desert Shield) having been replaced at the last minute by my best friend another captain, a Welfare, Recreation and Morale Commander, Tampa John.

While I avoided sand fleas and SCUD missile attacks and sweltering, nay, blistering heat, I supported the mission from stateside. After the war (Desert Storm) everyone came home and I met every flight. Later when the Air Force awarded me with the Bronze Star device, I summarily declined it as was my right, per regulations. Do not coddle me with your ribbons and bows.

One last example: I attended Officer Training School (OTS) as a 35 year old sergeant with 14 years of active duty service. I was assigned to the Pentagon at the time with the Joint Chiefs of Staff (JCS). I had been nominated by my cul-de-sac neighbor, the Secretary of the Air Force (SECAF), putting me in the terrible position of being a VIP nominee.

The (SECAF) serves at the pleasure of the president (Reagan) at the time, and wields authority over every general, even four star generals. It was a big endorsement given his *personal* recommendation. It's as if I was somebody, which I was not. I was just a young family man looking to climb the proverbial ladder within his organization. It was a long road just to be nominated and then selected for Officer Training School (OTS). I studied nights and weekends for 12 long years, due to my tours of duty, just to earn my four college degrees.

A minimum Bachelor's degree is required for officer hood. (See what I did there. I threw in '*hood*' so we can better relate.) I'll also try to find a way to insert 'crib' somewhere.

Being a VIP nominee maybe wasn't worth the price of admission. I caught a lot of flack over it. That's not the kind of attention you want in a military school meant to break you down and build you back up reshaping you into an elite United States Air Force Military Officer.

Most all other officer candidates were fresh out of college or about 22 years old. I'm just pointing out the age differences because with my enlisted rank and age, I was presumed a leader and shown great reverence and respect by these young whippersnappers fresh out of civilian life. Military bearing goes a long way in that environment.

At any rate, you can read all about my misadventures, being bed-posted, branded, demoted, black boarded (epaulettes) and crimes committed by active duty training officers and commanders, lies, deceit, conspiracies, (real ones not fake) and expulsion on graduation day of all days, and eventual reinstatement based on the findings of the Inspector General and the Air Force Board of Military Corrections. Again, and remember this, *the pen is mightier than the sword,* as demonstrated in my upcoming novel, **OTS**. A surefire must read for any young person thinking about joining the military but namely, the USAF.

So, while in class at OTS, I noticed a redheaded male cadet picking his nose in class. This was disgusting. He would explore his nasal cavity, withdrawing his digit probe examining the remnants and then ... wait for it ... eat it!

I was so put off by this behavior (disgusted actually) I cornered him on the next break in the restroom and threatened him with the most sincere warning I could muster, that if I ever saw him doing that nasty habit again, I'd make sure he was expelled never receiving his commission, a most coveted award. He would not serve in my Air Force. It was conduct unbecoming an officer. It stained the uniform.

I can't honestly tell you what I would have done had the cadet been black! [Hence the red-headed reference.] And therein lies the rub.

Can you see how he, and most others, would have colorized this incident as a racist ambush when in fact, it was not.

It was '**BAD BEHAVIOR**' (in my humble opinion) a malfunction pure and simple and in my direct line of sight that screamed to be corrected. Maybe the next time you feel victimized because of your race, could there possibly be a different reason!? Such as, Bad Behavior?

Are you being rude and inconsiderate or just plain foolish? Are your actions interfering with another's right to decency, privacy, peace and quiet, etc.

Now to revisit my Halloween Lynching story: I would hate for the civilian populace to draw the conclusion that ALL Air Force members picked their noses and ate the proceeds or were as ignorant or insensitive as this lone enlisted military housing resident. Both incidents are clearly in poor taste and poor judgments.

Hanging a ghost [clad in blue jeans, shoes and a shirt with a hood {pillowcase} over its head] from his tree was an out and out racist act in my opinion. That shamed my profession, uniform, branch of service, medals and all that I stood for. It mattered to me as a human being.

But it was a lone act by an individual, which leads me to my next point.

Stereotyping

We mustn't 'stereotype' but rather keep a clear distinction when judging anyone. I am unclear of his home of record. If from the South, he definitely knew better and was in fact, pushing the envelope. A complaint was lodged. The problem was resolved. He suffered no repercussions—a failure to lead in my opinion. It was out of my hands.

In social psychology, a stereotype is an over-generalized belief about a particular category of people. It is an *expectation* that people might have about every person of a particular group. The type of expectation can vary; it can be, for example, an expectation about the group's personality, preferences, or ability. That ALL (or most) cops are bad, or that ALL (or most) black people are dirty or bad or that ALL (or most) Mexicans are drug lords, criminals or carry diseases, or that ALL (of most) Jews are stingy, that ALL (or most) Asians drive badly, or that ALL (or most) white people live privileged lives or are above the law. It goes on and on and on.

When you stereotype you do a great disservice to your own shallow intellect, life travels and life experiences. All Muslims are not evil. They are different inasmuch as their belief system is different. Not wrong or right, just different.

No wait, they are wrong in many areas of human rights. But they don't believe in human rights. That's how kings and men over there roll. It is a learned behavior. Uncivilized? They still use goat heads as soccer balls. Come on. (Fact or fiction?)

ALL LGBTQ "Lesbian, gay, bisexual and transgender," the Q can stand for "questioning" -- as in still exploring one's sexuality -- or "queer," are in fact genetically different or have made a conscience choice to live a particular lifestyle, which is their right. They are not an abomination, especially if you believe in God, who has never made a mistake in his life. That you don't agree with God, is a judgment day conversation you can (and will) have later. Maybe don't like the *mechanics* of it all but don't hate the person. Everyone deserves to be respected.

Now, you have every right not to like something that is different. Let's take the lima bean for instance. To look at it, you might not like its size, shape or color for that matter. But if you've never tasted a lima, how do you truly know if you like it or don't like it. Get the facts. Don't judge indiscriminately.

Okay, now that we've establish that ALL lima beans truly are nasty, don't let that belief system taint the ever delicate sweet and delicious green pea.

If you don't like someone, that is your right. You should never let that hatred or dislike confuse you where the line is and if you are in business, open to the public, you can't discriminate against anyone you don't personally like. Hate crimes are up and that's got to end. You don't need a false prophet in DC to lead you to self-righteousness. You will not always benefit from those in leadership postings. They can and do lead you astray. Look to others for answers.

The intensity of this nation has increased because of poor leadership. Many are taking their cues from bad leadership. Leaders have vision and are admired. One mustn't demand respect but rather command it. There is a difference.

As a civilized society, we must do better, be better. It could very well be learned through some test that you in fact are incapable of empathy or tolerance or patience or whatever else is keeping you from finding kindness. Maybe your soul is *black* for use of a better word. Why? Because 'black' is bad right? Wait, let's change that and go with, soulless. And a cup of Joe is not to be taken 'black' but rather plain. We must stop associating 'black' as bad or wrong or evil.

We've got to address our subtle lexicon in ways that improve our understanding, appreciation and admiration of others.

Nigger: There really shouldn't be a DOUBLE STANDARD. If nigger truly is an ethnic slur, a **bad** word, then it ought not be allowed or permitted in black culture either.

Mouths should be washed out with soap every time it is uttered. Don't lay it on too thick that it's okay in one culture but not another. Freedom of Speech is protected but there are certain words which incite and are in poor taste. It is used with affection for instance amongst the African American community.

Changing rap songs to the N word simply loses its intended effect. It does not rhyme or cadence well.

Usage alert about nigger: The term nigger is now probably the *most* offensive word in the English language. Its degree of offensiveness has increased markedly in recent years. I would beg to differ. Cunt is likely the winner here.

This is a very slippery slope indeed. We either have Freedom of Speech protected under the

Constitution or we don't. We do not need ethic cleansings, racial epithets or restrictions on the press or freedom of speech, as is the practice throughout the world.

An epithet is a byname, or a descriptive term, accompanying or occurring in place of a name and having entered common usage. It has various shades of meaning when applied to seemingly real or fictitious people, divinities, objects, and binomial nomenclature.

The word "dirty" for example can be used as an epithet. **An adjective or descriptive phrase expressing a quality characteristic of the person or thing mentioned. "Old men are often unfairly awarded the epithet "dirty.""**

Civility and decency ought to be the better practice of community.

Civility comes from the word civics, which in Latin means "citizen." Merriam Webster defines civility as civilized conduct or a polite act or expression. Historically, civility also meant training in the humanities.

Let's ALL practice more civility.

Pardon Power

Another thing that riled me during my military career is a belief system that rank has its privileges. Not inasmuch as better food or quarters or better pay, which it does, but rather when it came to discipline: More often than not, the higher the rank, the less punishment received. More officers received slaps on the wrist where lower enlisted grades paid the price.

Executive pardon power, in my opinion, ought to be saved and used for the incarcerated who were wrongly convicted not the higher ranking governors or president's men who lied to Congress, committed crimes, admitted guilt on multiple accounts, were found guilty and sent to prison.

Pardons ought not be meant as 'Get out of Jail' FREE cards or passes. It's an abuse of power to do otherwise.

Remember, whomever you vote for says MORE about you than any candidate.

Even the most diabolical person will have followers and believers—the late and sick Charlie Manson for instance. The point here isn't cult leaders per se but those who follow blindly.

I would suspect something similar occurs in the law enforcement culture. Cops truly do believe they are not accountable to the public for their actions and are in fact, above the law. While they swear an oath to uphold the law, they, for some odd reason, do not believe that includes them.

There are many levels of protection—a herd of blue that surrounds and protects bad cops from all manner of offenses. Yes, even Cold Blooded Murder!! (Let that sink in for a moment.) If only cops understood that by weeding out and convicting bad cops, who are in fact, bad people, it would strengthen their forces and community prestige. Policing would be made safer for everyone. It would be a more honorable profession to aspire to for youth.

Most police officers throughout our nation needs retraining today. Tomorrow is too late. A badge is not a license to kill. 99.99% of cops do righteous policing. Being in the field putting their lives on the line, seeing the seediest sides of humanity, the underbelly if you will, I'm afraid ALL cops are hardened. If action were swifter against law enforcement for bad acts, it would send a meaningful, tangible signal.

Cops by their very nature are primal creatures. They thrive on 'action.' Streets are dangerous!! They also are peacekeepers. Many really do have a Service Heart. Most are proud beyond believe and as loyal as it gets—though oftentimes that loyalty is wrongly misplaced.

It is their nature to protect "themselves" first, be very clear on that. And because the public at large does NOT seem to heed their warnings to comply, as if it were a multiple choice question, force is used! There comes a point when all the bantering ends and you are taken to the ground.

Do not give them that opportunity or reason. Your very life depends on it. Things happen quickly in the street, more so if a Rookie cop has an itchy trigger finger or a tired knee needing a good place to rest it. Say, on a soft neck.

Holding you on the ground for more than 30 seconds while the restraints are being applied is long enough. You also have to understand, bad guys try to kill cops every single shift, day in and day out. They would rather steal a life than behave. There are few gentleman convicts. So, when a life can be stolen in a twitch, cops must make sure the man or woman or child standing in front of them won't be able to steal this cop's life, not today anyway.

Let's see a national movement where MANNERS MATTER. Let's fly those banners from atop every building in the country, or painted at every intersection. Or CHARACTER MATTERS, INTEGRITY MATTERS or …RESPECT!

I recall seeing on the news this young black woman in a car who was stopped for a traffic infraction and refused to exit the vehicle. She just ranted and raved telling the cop he had no right to stop her or whatever. She was then forced out of the vehicle and taken to jail. She was found dead in her cell three days later. Suicide? Mentally ill?

[Sandra Bland was a 28-year-old African American woman who was found hanged in a jail cell in Waller County, Texas, on July 13, 2015, three days after being arrested during a traffic stop.]

Imagine a different outcome had she only obeyed the officer. Was she kind and polite? No, she was self-righteous, agitated and argumentative. We need to bring manners black.　I mean, back! Granted, mentally challenged people require a different approach. A thick cargo net comes to mind.

The large black gentleman in NYC was selling 'loose' cigarettes. He did not have to die! He must however share some responsibility in his own demise. He had a duty to himself and family to behave as a good citizen & respect "authority" and he ignored every command. Every action does not always have an equal or opposite reaction. He hemmed & hawed, did not comply, tried to explain, resisted authority. Once he challenged authority and enough was enough, he was taken to the ground by a 4' 9" cop with a Napoleon complex jumped on his back and applied a chokehold. This larger than life man had a gnat on his back choking the life out of him as he resisted further. One moment he was enjoying his life on the planet in the warmth and sunshine and the next, choked out. Choke holds should never be used to subdue. Because they kill.

Top brass leadership must be more innovative.

Eric Garner (September 15, 1970 – July 17, 2014) 43, father of six, was an African-American man. He was a horticulturist at the New York City Department of Parks and Recreation before quitting for health reasons. The New York City medical examiner's office Friday confirmed what demonstrators had been saying for weeks: A police officer's choke hold on a man being arrested for selling loose cigarettes killed him.

Eric Garner, 43, died July 17 after being confronted by police on Staten Island for allegedly selling cigarettes illegally. Officer Daniel Pantaleo jumped on the back of Eric and began choking him eventually dropping both to the ground.

During the encounter, Garner raised both hands in the air and told the officers not to touch him. Seconds later, a video shows an officer behind him grab the 350-pound man in a choke hold and pull him to the sidewalk, rolling him onto his stomach.

"I can't breathe! I can't breathe!" Garner said repeatedly, his cries muffled into the pavement. The cause of Garner's death was "compression of neck (choke hold),

The New York police officer accused of fatally choking Eric Garner in 2014 (5 years later) has been 'fired' and will not reeive his NYPD pension, Commissioner James O'Neill said in a statement. "It is clear that Daniel Pantaleo can no longer effectively serve as a New York City Police offer as he has lost the faith of the public.

Daniel Pantaleo needs to be in prison—for cold blooded murder in broad daylight! Witnessed by millions.

Two Tampa cops were killed (murdered) in their patrol car by a handcuffed criminal because he was handcuffed in the *front*. That prompted all future handcuffing to bring hands/arms behind the back. This one move alone is enough for some to act out. It is claustrophobic to others. The act of someone putting their hands on you to cuff you is not a friendly gesture. Cops are trying to protect their lives at this point. Be very clear, cops are usually quite frustrated at this point too and will no doubt embark a little street justice or tune you up. This is not right and until you start behaving better, they likely won't either. A good calf roping this isn't supposed to be.

Criminals' hands are deadly weapons inasmuch as they can grab a gun or knife and kill a cop in $1/100^{th}$ of a second! A suggestion of mine some years ago was for cops to implement using specially designed oversized boxing gloves w/o thumbs to impede the grabbing of or using a hidden weapon, gun, knife. Of course, they would also need to be tethered as many a criminal would undoubtedly take a swing at the officer's head.

If cops felt safer in a controlled environment, fewer in the field deaths or abuses will occur. This will not however end bigotry or street justice. Police transport vans driven by bad cops in a way to knock criminals around on the inside will continue until or unless there are severe consequences.

Kneeling on a person of interests' neck is a crime. Just as striking a person with a baton to get them to comply. It is a conundrum to be sure.

Rarely, if ever, do good people flood the streets looking for peace from criminal behavior. The focus is almost entirely laid at the feet of cops behaving badly. Not that the victim was engaged in criminal activity, only how that apprehension took place. How about a little outrage for crimes being committed?

Military officers take an honor oath upon commissioning.

To wit:

"I will not lie, steal, cheat or tolerate those who do."

More emphasis must be placed on this honor code. If adopted and implemented by the blue line with immediate and severe consequences for those who violate it, only then will we see improvement.

Cops are a brotherhood. That is their culture. They protect their own at all costs. This must change. Once cops *"police"* themselves, holding those accountable for bad behavior & stop *protecting* them, with their unions and reps and supervisors, only then will we experience a paradigm shift! It is NOT about defunding police departments. Maybe criminals should form a union demanding better treatment.

District Attorneys must also do their jobs better. A bad cop is a criminal so act like it. Do your job! Shed the uniform and their badges. Treat their criminal behavior as any other criminal. DA's also take an oath. Don't oaths mean anything anymore?

Cops who cross the proverbial line become criminals and should be dealt with accordingly. Hang them, put in front of a firing squad, gas chamber or drip, drip, drip chemicals in their veins as murdering cops in the same light of day as their crimes. Televise it & we might see a paradigm shift. Shooting a fleeing suspect in the back in cold blood is murder, regardless of the circumstances. Planting weapons, lying, staging crime scenes is abhorrent behavior and as equally criminal as it gets.

Everyone plays a part in where we are today. Cops, not all, but most, know they will be protected if they mess up in the field because of a longstanding Thin Blue Line of protection. It's as if they have diplomatic immunity or something. They do not. The Thin Blue Line condones murder by remaining silent. Protecting ignorant, Rambo aggressions or racist acts by cops must never be tolerated. It stains the uniform. It stains the badge. It stains the soul of our great nation.

Looting

How pathetic is your life looting a *Dollar Store*!? Up your game man!

Rioting & looting spits in the faces of these murdered black men, women and children! Knock it off. How shameful when black youth set fires, break store windows to what?

Grab a handful or shopping cart full of clothes, a six pack of beer, wine or whiskey, a television. It's criminal behavior that perpetuates your race as undisciplined, street 'thugs' for a better term.

You are not taking it to the *'Man'* but rather destroying your communities and shop owners who have done nothing wrong. Looters obviously don't care. They are not well educated or own a business themselves or even attend church services. They are nothing more than profiteers. They know right from wrong. Looting is an abomination of humanity in its worst form.

No-Knock Warrants MUST BE Outlawed!

Kathryn Johnston (June 26, 1914 – November 21, 2006) was an elderly Atlanta, Georgia, woman who was killed by undercover police officers in her home on Neal Street in northwest Atlanta on November 21, 2006, where she had lived for 17 years. Three officers had entered her home in what was later described as a 'botched' drug raid. Officers cut off burglar bars and broke down her door using a no-knock warrant. Police said Johnston fired at them and they fired in response; she fired one shot out the door over the officers' heads and they fired 39 shots, five or six of which hit her. None of the officers were injured by her gunfire, but Johnston was killed by the officers. Police injuries were later attributed to friendly fire from each other's weapons.

One of the officers planted marijuana in Johnston's house after the shooting. Later investigations found that the paperwork stating that drugs were present at Johnston's house, which had been the basis for the raid, had been falsified. The officers later admitted to having lied when they submitted cocaine as evidence claiming that they had bought it at Johnston's house. <u>Three officers were tried for manslaughter and other charges surrounding falsification and were sentenced to ten, six, and five years</u>.

Breonna Taylor
After weeks of protests in Louisville inspired by the police killing of 26-year-old Breonna Taylor in her home, the city council unanimously voted on Thursday to ban local law enforcement from using "no-knock" warrants, which allow officers to enter a home unannounced.

The 26 local officials who represent districts in the state's largest city voted to pass "Breonna's Law," which also requires police and corrections officers to wear body cameras while serving warrants. Officers did not wear their cameras during the March shooting that killed Taylor, an emergency room technician studying to be a nurse.

"Breonna, that's all she wanted to do was save lives," Taylor's mother, Tamika Palmer, said at a news conference after the council vote. "With this law, she'll get to continue to do that. So, we're grateful for that. She would be so happy."

Taylor was killed during a police raid that started with a no-knock warrant. Plainclothes officers entered Taylor's home just after midnight on March 13. Taylor's boyfriend, Kenneth Walker, who lived with her, said he did not realize that the officers were police and fired one shot that hit a police sergeant's leg. Taylor was shot at least eight times and killed when officers opened fire in response.

Police have said they knocked before forcing entry into the home with a battering ram, but witnesses have disputed that claim. The warrant did not require the officers to make their presence known.

No officers have been Arrested or Charged in Taylor's death.

The **no-knock warrant** was part of a narcotics investigation, but neither Taylor nor Walker had prior drug convictions or arrests, and no drugs were found in the home. Although the primary targets of the investigation were allegedly operating more than 10 miles from Taylor's home, a judge signed a no-knock warrant to allow police to search her apartment because they believed one suspect had received packages at the address. The postal inspector police cited to justify the warrant has since said police did not contact his office, and a previous inquiry about Taylor's address found "no packages of interest going there."

The city council vote formalizes and extends a temporary ban instituted by Louisville Mayor Greg Fischer (D) on May 29 in response to protesters' demands.

Sen. Rand Paul (R-Ky.) introduced federal legislation Thursday that would outlaw no-knock warrants in virtually every jurisdiction in the country. Paul said he was spurred to sponsor the legislation after having conversations with Taylor's family.

"It's long past time to get rid of no-knock warrants," Paul said in a statement. <u>The Justice for Breonna Taylor Act</u> would ban federal law enforcement agencies from using no-knock warrants, and also require any local police agency that receives money from the Justice Department to comply with the ban.

In addition to the local ban on no-knock warrants, public outcry over the deaths also resulted in the police chief being fired and the governor ordering a review of the investigation into Taylor's death.

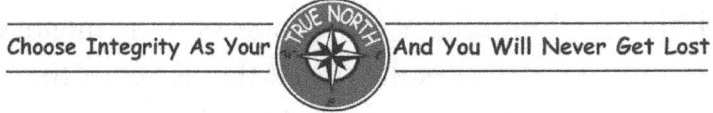

Voter Suppression

The next greatest dangers facing our nation are the growing numbers of Americans following the lies and ignorance found in Conspiracy Theorists. Their words, websites, podcasts, scenarios, contrived hypothesis and the like, create doubt and sow tribal chaos and destruction along with an endless trail or perpetuation of lies, and mass hysteria. These are the true 'thugs' in our society. Anyone [political party or person] who supports Voter Suppression for example, is a coward. They surely are not Americans or Patriots but rather China/Soviet-minded Communists deserving of their citizenship being revoked. They are a disgusting blight on humanity, a disgrace of the highest order!

Voter suppression is plain and simple: cheating. It has no place in America the Beautiful. The *will* of the people is our greatest gift to the process in this experiment we call democracy within our Republic. Voter suppression is meant to not only skew the results (stack the deck) of the people's voice but to downright make sure the house wins. It can never be allowed. Those who willing support voter suppression are our greatest enemy as mentioned in the oath of our leaders, to wit: "…any enemies, foreign or domestic…"

I do solemnly swear (or affirm) that I will support and defend the Constitution of the United States against all enemies, foreign and domestic; that I will bear true faith and allegiance to the same; that I take this obligation freely, without any mental reservation or purpose of evasion; and that I will well and faithfully discharge the duties of the office on which I am about to enter: So help me God

Georgia Voter Suppression is sickening, racist, ignorant, a federal crime and yet the GOP and Governor condone it.

Twitter banned me (yesterday) for tweeting this harmless yet innovative idea how to best resolve the ballot box voter suppression issue plaguing our democracy. An idea I believe has merit. One that eliminates 5+ hours standing in lines to vote or polling places being closed by the hundreds making it more difficult to vote, etc.

The idea is to repurpose **ATM**s nationwide to serve as [**Pin Access Ballot Boxes**] capturing photos, ID, pin number, and down ballot votes cast, then locks it up tight! No ability to vote twice. Once a pin is used once, that's it.

Was this really worth banning me Jack Dorsey?

Oregon is but one state which votes exclusively by mail. Voting by mail has never been a problem in the 25+ years I've lived here. Reviewing a ballot at my kitchen table is a wonderful thing as it affords me the time to make my thoughtful decisions. A voter's pamphlet arrives weeks before the ballot so everyone has plenty of time to read it. I don't actually mail in my ballot but rather drop it off at the court house in the special "white' ballot mail box just outside the court house. My ballot is never lost in the mail.

Those dangerous conspiracy theorists or 'thugs' as they shall forever be referred to, are dead wrong about voter fraud or changing the outcome of an election because mail-in ballots were permitted. They deploy 'scare' tactics to frighten you. Like bad demons coming from south of the border to rape you. Dear God, wise up America. You're giving public schools a bad name. I have to wonder, when did people stop thinking for themselves? Americans can't be this dumb/ignorant.

Besides, whomever you vote for says more about **you** than any candidate!

Why we're at it, I would end the Electoral College. It's not right when a few states can elect our Ruler. When votes in 30+ states don't matter, that's a problem! Our beloved Founding Fathers didn't get everything right. Why else Amendments to our Constitution? Read them. Giving women the 'right' to vote took until 1920 (ratified) 19th Amendment.

Assigning Labels

Racism. You really shouldn't blame this on the Crips and Bloods or any gang affiliation. Discrimination is in all our DNA. It's a flight or fight response. One bad experience can skew your thinking in absolutes forever. If you had one bad experience with a person of color, it's likely you will judge ALL persons of colors badly. This is known as stereotyping. This is the mindset that keeps us from thinking independently, rationally, reasonably, intelligently. Steer clear of absolutes. Nothing is ALL good or ALL bad. Don't let bad past experiences hold you hostage to enlightenment.

Bringing slaves to America is our nation's greatest sin unto itself. (Bombing Japan's cities of Hiroshima and Nagasaki to end Word War II was another.) When a nation is at war, it's very common for its citizens to physically loathe the enemy's people. Japanese were treated horrifically based on the war effort, their culture, appearance, and wartime atrocities. Japanese American citizens living in America were rounded up and interred in prison camps until the war effort ended. Talk about your civil rights! These were citizens. Marching on Portland or Seattle or DC by young people, really need to read their history. You think you've been violated, dream on.

I personally hate it when our lexicon gets hijacked by some group. Gay used to be a perfectly wonderful expression of gaiety. We have been robbed of its primary usage. Before this 'thug thang' gets out of hand…before we lose yet another *word* to activists, racists, or editorial suggestions (with or without intent, malice or agendas), because it's convenient or furthers their cause, giving them purpose, keeping them in business, before we lose yet another black child from a bullet thrown from a white man's right to stand his ground law or a black gang member who only knows street justice; before we widen the racial gap further than it is, I want to invite a responsible national debate on this new 'thug' meaning.

Not that long ago, 24 mug shots cover my 65 inch big screen *color* television with the arrest of a New Jersey carjacking ring who pistol whipped and killed at least one victim. Millions of dollars worth of high-end vehicles carjacked in New York and New Jersey, en-route to Africa, and what ratio do you, as an informed reader, would surmise were 'black?' Venture a guess; an educated one. See if you are biased; NONE! I present this scenario because it lines up with Mr. Pitt's article and a test for his readers.

Some in the media are trying to assign 'thug' improperly. Let's stop that nonsense. There is entirely too much hate in this country.

What's more dangerous for you, your family, your children, your parents, grandparents, friends, and your way of life: American Arrogance or American Ignorance? I don't believe they are mutually exclusive. Will we ever evolve enough to accept people for who they are or because of their differences? How do you hate Asians but love Chinese or Thai food? How do you hate Mexicans, some of the hardest workers I have ever encountered in my days working in the fields, and yet enjoy their restaurants, lawn care?

This is a great opportunity for us, for you, for me, for them, to stop it dead in its tracks by not allowing those who would promote or suggest this word now be assigned to black youth. We can hold these spreaders of racist igniters accountable before their meaning takes hold. Once we refuse to label, we can begin to heal as a nation.

My publisher called upon author Mike McCune to *drum* up a brief, yet thorough, paper on the origins of 'thug' which I found fascinating. Please don't overlook the history on the true meaning at the beginning of this book. Oh, and by 'drum' up I don't mean anything tribal by it. Words! Words matter!

'thug' becoming the new racial slur is definitely positioning itself for a candid debate. My rambling thesis puts forth the idea that those who would knowingly use their national platforms to suggest or assign 'thug' as a new racial slur, are being highly inflammatory, irresponsible and asinine.

The meaning, as an undertone or overtone, no matter how subtlety applied, or openly, or how politically correct you may think it is, is divisive and destructive and does a great disservice to young black youth everywhere. We must rail against creating or fostering stereotypical mindsets for the intended target of this new hate jargon, which includes all black youth and black men. This is unacceptable. I also find it odd that a black syndicated columnist would put forth such a proposal, planting the seeds as it were. Though, as I have learned, it was white newspaper editors who assigned his article's title. And there you go.

There is already a great racial undercurrent dividing this nation, which has been percolating for years. When our top executive is a race baiting bigot, well, it's all to expected. We may be just one word away from striking and igniting the tinderbox for an all out race war. Adopting 'thug' as hate of young black kids is going to have more deadly consequences. We see the manifestations in our nightly news night after night.

Something few years back demonstrates just how much mental illness or mental instability exists in our nation. Michael Dunn, 47, a Florida software developer is now convicted of attempted murder. Testimony revealed he hates *thug* music and fired ten, count them, X, 10 shots into a car of four black teens, **killing** Jordan Davis, 17, for playing their loud *thug* music and otherwise being argumentative when asked to turn down their music. (A mistrial on the murder charge.) Really? Mr. Dunn felt it was okay to kill *thugs*. Unimaginable! You can't call a bullet back, let alone ten of them. And pay attention here: A gun is NO MORE responsible for murder and mayhem than a pencil is for a misspelling.

A law-abiding person calls police IMMEDIATELY afterwards not the local pizza parlor. Christsakes. How a jury did not convict of Mr. Dunn of murder speaks volumes to just how badly the lines are being blurred.

Trayvon Martin, 17, killed by George Zimmerman, because George thought he *looked* suspicious, no doubt, 'looking' like a *thug* when it's pretty clear, this self-anointed neighborhood patrolman was looking for trouble/confrontation. A young black *thug* in the hoodie—which he found. Mr. Zimmerman deserves the chamber. How did we get so soft?

Can we afford to allow this *thug* mentality to bleed into the fabric of America. We may never get the stain out as it is.

Google: 30 year old killed by police in (insert city).

Google: 20 year old killed by police in (insert city).

Google: Know their names: Black people killed by police in the US. Results: Between 2014 and 2019, the PoPo KILLED 6,557 people! Guess how many were BLACK?

Talk about duck season! Law Enforcement and politicians have failed us all. Vote them **ALL** out. (In this case, going with 'absolutes' is perfectly okay.)

Retired Tampa police officer, Curtis Reeves Jr., 71 charged with fatally shooting Chad Oulson, 43, both white. Wait! Neither of these men is black? This begs the question: Can white men rate the *thug* moniker too? Answer: YES!

This isn't a black thing! It's not a Mexican thing. It's not an Asian thing. It's not a white thing. It's a BEHAVIOR thing.

Thug is NOT becoming (or should not) become a new racial slur.

Regarding the confrontation between Mr. Curtis Reeves Jr., 71 and Chad Oulson, 43, we have a perfect example of an unintended consequence to a preventable circumstance. Had Chad not been texting in a movie theater he'd be alive today. It really is **that** simple.

As a society, many young adults don't have the perspective of an older generation where manners matter.

Chad lacked situational awareness, which we all know is being disrespectful to others around him by texting in a movie theater and not respecting the request to respect the man asking for quiet. He allowed his uncouth machismo to get the better of him.

We all could make this a teachable moment for this lesson and other lessons we are receiving in this new normal, as wake-up calls (warnings) for not only what can happen, what does happen. I think the kids call it being "Woke."

In an instant, Chad's wife and daughter are without the man of their dreams—forever, and for what? Nothingness is a horrific state of reality. So Chad doesn't die in vain, maybe you can think of others and how your actions are affecting them the next time you are being rude or more likely, oblivious to your surroundings. If someone asks you to move, be quite, stop tailgating, or whatever, at the very least, take a beat before responding. You could be right and you could be dead right.

While we may never be able to extinguish hate, we must endeavor to thwart the prevailing 'arrogance of entitlement' or attitudes of superiority or whatever it is which embodies generations of bad behavior. The country, nay the world, is becoming a more dangerous place because of this selfishness. Strive instead for "Selflessness."

    Had Curtis not been so irritated or annoyed by the actions of Chad texting or likely Chad's smart-ass reply when asked to stop texting, thank God Chad wasn't black or he might well have been shot right there on the spot—and for what—for just being a ruthless texting *thug*? As we all know, no one likes that loud *thug* texting, music, gangster behavior.

    Mr. Reeves had many opportunities to reposition himself in the theater, and yes, he had every right to remain in the seat he had previously marked as his own territory. Management was also arguably neglect by not intervening when Mr. Curtis left his seat seeking assistance for the rude movie patron who was texting, seated in front of him. The manager was likely only 17 years old her or himself.

Mr. Reeves was already growing highly agitated, whether he was of sound mind or not doesn't matter at this point. He was boiling and being a former cop, his attitude as to what to expect was already established. By God, if this person in front of me doesn't listen to my commands, I'll make sure he does. Pulling out his gun and shooting Chad, was about the height of arrogance and stupidity that can exist in a confrontation which in bygone years would have been nothing more than poke in the nose, a scuffle, or an all out wrestling match.

Either way, popped corn was going to be spilled. The fact that blood was spilled and hearts were broken, ought to serve as a loud siren of silence or beacon of light (or darkness) that something more has to be done with humanity and prevent these ever-increasing incidents of horror.

~

Maybe, just maybe, pushing back against assigning 'thug' as the new racial slur is one way we can start to heal or change the process. I'm confident every reader of this book [both of you] will have their own opinions too. We need that. Don't agree or disagree with me, pick up your own banner to improve this country.

Had Chad, in all his entitled arrogance, not reached over his seat and grabbed a box of popcorn out of Curtis' hand, in a quick and threatening manner, then throwing it back in Mr. Reeves' face, assault and battery in itself, who's to say what the outcome would have been? An educated guess is that Chad would still be reading bedtime stories to his three year old daughter had he himself been a little more polite; or treated his elders with a modicum of respect.

I'm absolutely positive that when Chad went to the movies that afternoon, he never thought, even for a nanosecond, he'd be shot and killed over an argument with a stranger. The absurdity is deafening and yet so predictable nowadays.

This is PRECISELY the point I'm trying to make here: Think Beyond the Act.

By this I mean, what might the consequence be for your action (Act)? You must program yourself to condition your response when an event presents itself. It takes discipline. It takes courage. It takes thoughtfulness and intelligence. Beating one's chest is so last year. If you feel threatened or challenged, having previously placed yourself in possible scenarios, thinking them through and all the variables and possible outcomes, only then can wisdom and a calm demeanor have a chance to prevail. Apologize and live. The more we engage in escalated conversations, the more tragedies.

The key here is to defuse the situation, not escalate it. Defuse. You can live to tell your stories rather than have people remember you with theirs…

Life is a precious thing. It's not a dress rehearsal.

If a situation does happen and you've adopted this premise of thinking beyond the act, you will react with a more measured response than to a knee-jerk, over reaction. This could save your life.

There are no excuses whatsoever for Chad to have grabbed this older gentleman's popcorn from his hands and throw it back in his face. That sole act of aggression got him killed, not the texting. Chad has to own that!

Had Chad trained himself to Think Beyond the Act, and conditioned himself not to act on impulse, or impulsively, or with such aggression, considering there may not always be truth in Newton's third law: *for every action, there is an equal and opposite reaction*…because the truth is, it's usually worse—horribly worse.

Had Chad chose a different option, the outcome would have surely been less devastating for everyone. Look at the consequences of Chad's action. Did he deserve to be murdered? Of course not, but that's exactly what can happen. He was butting heads with a total stranger unaware how unstable and impulsive this **former bad cop** was.

<u>THINK BEYOND THE ACT</u>. How you do this is to take a beat in the moment. Pause and consider you options. Seconds matter. It keeps you from overreacting or acting out impulsively and could save your life. Think of the consequences of your actions. Be more polite, less aggressive and argumentative.

Chad absolutely should have shown this request to stop texting with more consideration, more respect, especially since it was coming from a senior citizen and just turned off his cell phone or leave his seat and make the call from the lobby— all far better options. Don't be a Chad! And definitely don't be a Curtis! Show restraint, unless you are unstable. Then the best laid advice gets washed down the drain into the sewer.

Chad was likely so cocksure of his 'right' to make his text, he likely didn't take to kindly to the 'suggestion' to behave accordingly. My guess is, had his mother leaned in and asked him to turn off his cell phone, or a manger, or anyone else in authority, he would have. Bravado is a deadly fuse.

And yes, it is sometimes the 'way' you ask that matters. Though, more and more people are not recognizing any form of authority. Why? Because they have this mindset where they will do as they damn well please, damn the consequences. Reap what you sew, I suppose.

We need less aggressive individuals; less aggressive moments; less governments and nations in general. Our entire culture is aggressive.

People aren't exercising their options. Shooting into a car of young boys goes beyond insane and is itself 'thuggish' and yet it's normal given the mindsets of some. There was not imminent threat to loss of life. A *thug* would have surely fired upon him, had there been a gun in the car. These young men were just playing loud music. See now none of it makes sense. That's rather the brilliant point. It rarely ever does make sense.

How do we make this world a better place?

Grace is how…

It starts with you. Appeal to your higher angels. If you are not religious, then appeal to your higher intelligence. Find your common sense. It's not in your boot. Do not escalate, but rather be braver and defuse a situation. Take pride in doing that. There is true satisfaction if you can walk away; apologize.

Recognition of your behavior or that it is offending someone speaks to where the line may be. It is likely bad enough or socially unacceptable if you are being asked to keep it down or slow down or stop tailgating or whatever.

Think how it must take real courage in today's world to even speak up. But if we don't speak up, bad behavior will continue running unchecked. And that's no way to maintain a civilized society. Policing each other is problematic at best. Wearing your Covid-19 mask doesn't hurt anyone's ears, or bother them in any way—that is to say, unless they have been programmed to 'hate' masks, ergo, the politicizing of masks.

How small-minded have we become!?

I've seen segments on the news where grown-ass adults are throwing hissy fits and tantrums because the store is requiring them to wear a mask. For christsakes people, pull it together. Thank God it's mandatory for surgeons to don their masks, for as much as 10+ hours. So stop whining. I saw where one guy reaches out and rips the mask from another. That will likely get him shot nowadays. Another, self-anointed Mask Patrol was shaming a group just trying to order their meals who were not wearing masks. A fight ensued putting the Mask Patrol senior on his butt. Take any lesson from this you choose.

Don't flex your muscles and fight back. Accept the 'suggestion' and do the right thing. You already know what it is…if you don't, educate yourself.

An older white lady entering a store took her cane and batted it at this black woman for not wearing a mask and got herself knocked on her ass. You can't make this stuff up.

Know that your breastfeeding may offend someone. It shouldn't but it may. You have rights, and so do others. That's usually the point lost on offenders. Don't be so arrogant or focused on yourself that you lose that nugget of sense. When in a public setting, behave accordingly. When you're at home, do whatever you please.

Rules of etiquette STILL apply; whether you agree or not. Others do. What's perhaps happening is, people are taking their private lives out into public and not modifying their behavior. People expect you to behave appropriately and accordingly. You are not living in a Hippy commune. Talking loudly on your smartphone isn't very smart. Texting while driving puts us at in peril. You are endangering our lives. We have a right to defend ourselves when you come at us with your head down.

I fear long gone are the days of civility. Don't know what that word means. Look it up.

Character Matters

Manners Matter

Having integrity means doing the 'right' thing *even* if no one is looking. Think what that means. You have to be the person who does the right thing because it's the right thing. If this were our credo, we'd make the human race prouder.

I had a first cousin, Alana, 26, and mom to two beautiful boys, killed by a speeding bandit in a horrific automobile crash. It was NOT an accident. It was a very preventable circumstance had the thug not just robbed a store and fleeing police at a high rate of speed.

A niece rear-ended a car while she was texting; another niece was read-ended by tailgating, texting maniacs.

I've had a brother enter a nine (9) day coma with permanent brain trauma when he was only 19 because some young 'white' thug ran a red light.

I had another brother struck as a pedestrian also in Seattle suffering a broken 'everything' and undergoing many operations and three hip replacements to date. On the 'Richter' scale of severe and excruciating pain for much of his life, all because of a moment, a split second, of inattentive driver.

My middle son lost his car to a young white meth addict who was driving 'high' running red lights in town. The story has a better ending. He was only 15, at the time, saved his money to buy a used Mercedes diesel. As his protective father, I rather enjoyed his having a heavy duty hardened bunker on wheels. He waited one full year to save more money for his car insurance. Finally the day came. He drove it to get fuel and then to the salon to get his hair styled as any 16 year old boy with his first car would. As he left the shop looking all dapper, he noticed his car had been hit and shoved forward a few parking spaces thereby hitting the parked car in front of it. His 'brand new' car was crushed on both ends. It now looked like a Renault. He was devastative. But he was safe.

The punk hit and run driver sped away, also hitting more cars and hurting other drivers who were unfortunately behind the wheels of their cars as they passed through the carefree intersection on a warm, sunny day having the green light.

Luckily, I followed up the leads witnesses provided and identified him from a convenience store video where he had stopped two miles up the road for smokes and a soda. I then turned the information over to police and he was arrested. He was maybe not a thug but he is an idiot.

I made sure my young, impressionable son was present at the courthouse when this white 'idiot/thug' was arraigned and later sentenced for driving recklessly (in his grandmother's car) no less. Thankfully, she had insurance, because she is not a thug and is responsible, and my son received a full settlement for his totaled car of less than one mile traveled. The point to all of this is we all have to deal with 'thugs' (bad behavior) on a daily basis. If we are to assign 'thug' to anyone, let it be anyone who behaves badly. Hooligan is just too tame.

When you don't behave appropriately, you can be sure someone (probably with a gun) will hold you accountable. That's just the law of the land anymore. So is it really worth being an ass?

Look up from your texting while walking across the street; turn off your phones while driving or in airplanes and restaurants. Grow up. Be more considerate.

Stop multitasking while driving. You are putting other people's lives in danger—people with families, many have children. Don't boom, boom your music while driving with windows down. Be...wait for it... considerate! Be considerate of those around you. In other words, don't be a thug. I want for us to label Bad Behavior 'thuggish' not a specific race. That's the point here.

It's important to learn from these 'preventable' tragedies so these people don't die in vain or unnecessarily. Or so you or someone you know doesn't perish from this earth too soon. These are not accidents. Be very clear on that. They do not just happen for happenstance stake. They are very preventable situations which escalate with deadly consequences. (Yes, you are being lectured. Get over it. Deal with it.)

Is American behavior devolving? Seattle, Portland, Washington DC and other major cities would have you believing yes, yes it is. Are the developmental and intelligence levels of generations decreasing as a whole? Are manners eroding? Do you honestly not know where the line is anymore?

Have parents been neglectful in passing down manners, teaching proper social behavior, instilling good values? Or are these isolated, headline grabbing, incidents the new normal? I guess once you burn down your city, you fully expect it will be rebuilt. Think again. Many inner cities won't. Decay sets in and people move out. You have in effect, pissed on your home.

For as progressive or as enlightened as we want to think of ourselves, as individuals or a society, attitudes are changing with each unfolding generation from selflessness to selfishness in a mantra that puts us decades behind where we could be if we only thought differently. If only we had true mentorship. The problem is we tend to emulate the actions of others. And those actions or role models are not always ideal.

Of course, I believe there are far more people who know how to behave. You are not therefore a thug by definition.

Technology has been stellar at improving or enhancing our lives but it has also unplugged us from reality and from one another. We bury our heads in screens more than we look for smiles or twinkles in eyes or stars. We walk around in our own world oblivious to our surroundings or how we might be impacting others. Frankly, because we just don't give a damn. This has to change.

The more we devolve into an uncaring society, the less we accomplish and the more hostility we exert upon others. Is this really where you want to be heading? Did the creators of Mad Max get it right? I hope not. That's one lame world. And it's so dusty. If you have children, is this the crazy world they will live in? Put your foot down now. Stand up for change—under your roof and under society's awning.

Write to Senators, Congressmen and Congresswomen. Write to automakers to install cell blocking devices while cars are moving. (GPS work this way.) Stop this two ton bullet from launching into you or your child.

Let's SLOW DOWN 16 year old drivers.

A mechanical **governor** uses flyweights to create a force based off of crankshaft speed which is balanced by the force of the **governor** spring. ... The interaction of the **governor** spring and mechanical **governor** holds the throttle at the desired engine rpms based upon a force balance and the load / operating conditions. Hello. It's not rocket science.

Gang violence must end. In cases such as these, shooting someone is such a permanent solution to a temporary problem. I know you've heard this before. People need to start recognizing their options. Take away guns and maybe gangs will start stabbing each other. Take away knives and maybe gangs will start boxing. Maybe boxing will lead to broken noses, black eyes and gold medals instead of daily funerals and tombstones.

Hmmm.

I so believe in this country, its people and our way of life. I know with the right leadership, the correct vision and implementation of ideas, we can outshine any nation as ours will become a nation of humanity, innovation, togetherness and culture. What you need to understand is, we all have a shadow self. A side we never show anyone. I'm neither a politician nor a lawyer—thank God! I am a Wordsmith. I think the regular people of other nations are more like us than we know, admit, or care to acknowledge. Where it gets twisted is how those masses of people are led by few, ourselves included. There are some 300 million of us and only 500+ of them. How did we permit this?

How did we allow them to screw up our country so badly? I truly believe we need new leadership the world over. How we get there is one step at a time with each of us looking at what is possible not what isn't.

Many younger generations may have never heard the immortal words of John F. Kennedy when he spoke of selflessness. We need to get back to that.

John F. Kennedy's inaugural address inspired children and adults to see the importance of civic action and public service. His historic words, "**Ask not** what your country can do for you – **ask** what you can do for your country," challenged every American to contribute in some way to the public good.

As a nation, we are SO lacking in leadership. I was fortunate to hear his younger brother speak, and get his autograph. #RFK.

I get so frustrated with the way our government operates it is maddening at times. There are many things which do work, and so I concentrate on those that don't. I think we have too many *smart* people running our country. It's time for regular people to be represented. I think truth and common sense ought to prevail, not backroom deals.

I feel with those two cornerstones as our foundation, we stand a better chance of success than anything currently being offered. I think it's high time the working middle class have a real voice and enjoy a far better and much higher standard or quality of living.

Restating it here!!! Our Forefathers didn't get all right, why else all the "Amendments" to our U.S. Constitution? And Congress certainly doesn't always get it right either. Did you know the U.S. Constitutional Amendment to give women the 'right' to vote failed to pass? Can you imagine had we had Social Media back then? Oh my word. Not until the 19th Amendment (1920) did women **win** the right to vote! I wonder if any of them ever protested in the streets? Nah, probably not.

All I'm saying is I didn't get everything right in this book either. I knowingly meandered into the weeds. I'm known for that. But as long as I have a captive audience, why not share some of my thoughts, right?

Brainstorming is where seeds are planted which can germinate if enough people agree with a particular vision for America the Beautiful. Instead of asking why I'm not running for office. Why aren't you? We have to take our country back. It's been in the hands of life-long politicians, aristocrats, millionaires and billionaires, conspiracy theorists, bullies and bigots far long enough.

Middle Class, rise up! Right those things you find wrong. It's truly the ONLY way anything will be accomplished.

"This book" with its awesome cover, is about standing up against the media or lame politicians or bad cops and not letting them push you into a corner. Do not let anyone assign a meaning to the word 'thug' as a racial slur on the backs of black youth.

Confrontations escalate quickly—oftentimes with deadly consequences. This much we know.

Whether it's selling loose cigarettes, or passing a counterfeit $20 bill, or just checking out a construction site, privileged, ignorant, arrogant, racists white men and bad cops must be held to a higher standard!

Cops swore an oath to protect and serve not pin a badge their chests giving them a license to kill. The shame, the unbridled terror, the gut wrenching pain for extended family members and friends, all put into motion in one heated moment of ego, arrogance and bullying neighborhood hoodlums, bad policing.

If **good cops** <u>refused</u> to <u>protect</u> **bad cops** from tarnishing their profession, we'd flip this crap on a dime. It's like when one or ten priests commit horrible sins against youth, when the church hides it, the cover up is as grave a sin. Just reassigning priests to another parish only condones the sin. It paints ALL priests as predatory—which is not the case.

The same is true for cops or any profession for that matter—military, veterans, medical professionals, teachers, etc., all do a disservice to their badges, oaths, character, honor, uniforms, legacies, by protecting criminals amongst them. When did this become okay? I don't get it.

My sole purpose for writing this book was to warn, advise or otherwise caution against assigning 'thug' to any race whatsoever but especially black youth. I freely admit, I landed in the weeds more than once. So be it.

Let's instead, if we must, assign it to *behavior*, plain and simple. Another purpose is to give young black youth and their parents some honest to goodness truths about how best to protect their children and themselves from Johnny Law. Don't fight and fuss. Though that doesn't always matter, bad cops will still stop you and take you to the ground, because they can. It's going to take real leadership at all levels of policing including police chiefs, police commissioners, politicians and cops themselves, to get to where we need to be.

Remember, I recently used the word *thug* myself for the first time in my life and it felt good. I'll reveal my usage later in this book.

Bullying is bad behavior that could be classified as being a thug. It has always been prevalent but it is now rearing its ugly head more often than is acceptable, manifesting with the ever-escalating nonsensical shooting deaths by whites on blacks. But not just blacks, black youths. At least Covid-19 has ended school shootings for a moment while we catch our collective breaths.

The think I want everyone reading this book to know is why school shootings happen in the first place. Beyond the attention getting adolescents, it stems from bullying.

Columbine was about bullying taken to the extreme. It is widely believed that Eric Harris and Dylan Klebold took revenge in the 1999 massacre of classmates and staff to even the score on schoolyard bullies who tormented them to the point of no return.

My own son KD was bullied so badly, so relentlessly in his Texas middle school, it was easily conceivable he too would have concluded this a satisfactory outcome to his daily brutal torture, heartache, ridicule, embarrassment and pain. Thank God, he is an old soul of incredible spirit and grace and reason, or I'd be writing an entirely different book.

At 6'5" 290 pounds, I've never been bullied as an adult. I can't say the same as a naïve, bright-eyed, fresh faced 10 year old skinny new kid on the block. The 8th grade was brutal. So many knee thrusts to the beanie sack it isn't funny.

I was born in Ashland, Oregon and my family moved around a lot, but I always found them again. The point is, I was the new kid at a lot of schools, Michigan Avenue middle school in Coos Bay, Oregon and oh brother did I get hazed. I didn't know it at the time what it was, but I was being bullied on a fairly regular basis by punks (thugs) and jocks. (Terms we all pretty much can agree on right?)

It was 1963 and times were different back then. We had one rotary, party-line phone hanging on the kitchen wall; three channels, no cable and no color television. We kids played outside all day, every day. We were all skinny, healthy and happy. I was not at all street wise growing up on the west side of Coos Bay in a little neighborhood known as Empire. My big mistake as the new kid at school was winning Punt, Pass and Kick, (PP&K) as a 10 year old. Well, that wasn't the mistake exactly, but besting the 11, 12 and 13 year olds was. Who knew, I was a phenom? Another *word* that hadn't been coined yet. Well, do you think this young prodigy continued excelling in the face of his schoolyard peers or suppressed in his excellence cowering instead in fright?

The jocks and punks would corner me in the boys' bathroom and lure me in close and sweet as if to befriend me or something and then with one very quick, stealthy move, knee me in the beanie sack. Time and time again, I fell for that prank. (I wasn't the sharpest pencil in the box.)

Everyone would laugh as I curled over in excruciating, agonizing, nauseating pain. Those bony knees really packed a punch. I recall the main perp, Murphy Brown. Cool name, but a punk all the same. He was a tough, intimidating kid.

I never told my teachers or parents. I mean how could I? In those days, even the *word* 'pregnant' was a nasty, forbidden, unspeakable *word*. Don't even get me started on douche. The verbalization we boys would say as we made our brothers and friends flinch and then socked 'em in the shoulder saying, douche, douche, and douche.

I never really understood my mother telling us boys not to say that *word*. I thought we invented it. Besides, and this is my point: that *word* had precisely NO MEANING to it whatsoever. None. Zero. It was just a cool sounding *word* whenever you landed a punch…douche!

So, the last thing this country needs is for those in the media, with a wide platform of influence and means, to perpetuate and endanger more black kids by classifying them as 'thugs' by assigning their own self-serving meaning (as a politically correct racial slur) to advance their stated or hidden agendas, thereby fostering 'open season' on thugs and more inevitable 'justifiable' homicides.

One of the highlights in my adolescence is when the Harlem Globetrotters came to town. Watching them perform their magic antics on the court is etched in my memory, man, that was so fun. Those guys were giants, funny and so talented. Coordination beyond believe. This was my second experience with black people. 100% positive.

My first experience was when I was five or six years old living in Klamath Falls, Oregon. I had a neighborhood friend. We were besties. I can't recall his name exactly, oh wait, it was Monty. He was black. He loved sucking on lemons. His family had me over to dinner where they served ham and watermelon. There was nothing assigned to that, just a typical normal family. I do have to admit, I thought Monty was an Indian. He was always correcting me, "Thomas, I'z not an Indian." I likely watched too many Westerns back then.

My third experience with black folk was in my 8th grade year. I was attending middle school in Coos Bay, Oregon. One day a group of black boys from Portland, Oregon came to our school. They stayed for one week with families in our community. Sort of an exchange program I believe.

Let me tell you this, there was NOT one *thug* among them. They were kind, nice, polite and funny as hell—definitely a class clown or two, as was I. Perhaps therein lies the bonding. They were sharp dressers and good athletes. Anyone one of them could have been my best friend.

I was fully prepared to embrace black people with open arms in my later years—the military for instance.

Where are the gentlemen, the mentors, the role models, the leaders and positive influencers nowadays?

Richie Incognito and Jonathan Martin of the Miami Dolphins, one white, one black. Ask yourself who's the '*thug*?' It ain't the black guy.

Bullying is a national crisis, an epidemic on an increasing scale from kindergarten to retirement homes, no doubt. As a reasoned and civilized nation, we must end bullying once and for all.

Maybe the next to the last thing we need in this country are leaders in business and government who bully. The arrogance and intimidation of such behavior and abuse of power warrants condemnation and consequence. Bullying in any form, by anyone, cannot be condoned, ignored or tolerated under any circumstances.

Mr. Pitts infers in his editorial that '*thug*' is becoming the new politically accepted racial slur, assigning '*thug*' specifically to black youth.

I immediately fired off an email to him where he states in his reply, that's not what he meant, necessarily.

Hmmm. Maybe if people said what they meant and mean what they say, we'd all be better informed. Attention grabbing headlines are by their very nature meant to stir emotions, ignite controversy. Mission Accomplished. I wrote most of this book in one sitting and published it years later. That's why some of it is so *dated* but those examples also illustrate just how little has changed. I would say things have gotten worse.

If the current trend is to assign 'thug' to a race, how about we stop that? How about each and every one of us take some responsibility here to think for ourselves and speak up when something doesn't feel right, sound right or make sense. Push back. Stand up. Speak out. Do not fall into the traps those in the media set. Don't buy into the fear mongering.

Creating Healthy Dialogue

Creating a healthy dialogue on the subject of racism shines light on it and perhaps, together, we can stomp out those who are inherently driven to increase the racial gap.

Miscommunication plays a highly significant role in our lack of understanding of each other, as does our varying life experiences, points of view and overall upbringing, education, exposure to role models and the like.

Repatriations

While I have you, let's discuss repatriations. Some might ask if repatriations haven't already been made.

The opportunities afforded black men, especially elite athletes, with combined earnings of $3T+ [trillion] including salaries, merchandizing, branding, licensing, endorsements, lifetime pension plans, investments, real estate and so forth. Might this actually be a jumping off point? Perhaps there could be some discussion on whether or not it is incumbent upon these gifted, anointed souls to give back to their roots, their communities, their race, by proxy. Many already do. Many professional athletes, including white athletes, with philanthropic hearts, do not see race in their giving.

Asking your government namely, taxpayers, to pay you personally for something that happened over 400 years ago is a big ask. Maybe sports fans have already footed the bill. 1619 was a long time ago. And it's a slippery slope. How do we as a society ever hope to endeavor to make right all the ills of our past? Do we subtract then from all the damage & destruction?

Toppling inanimate statutes will make you feel good in the moment, but it's not your job to deface monuments. That is the work of legislatures. Show your disdain in less critical mass ways. The imagery seeps into already racists' minds validating their belief system. How about voting in those of like-minds? That's our process in this country. Taking the law into your own hands is highly discouraged. Recall the KKK?

Law and Order sets us apart from other civilizations/nations. Rioters can topple these confederate structures of intolerance or we can do it the right way. Though, admittedly, it won't be as much fun. But still. Think of the images you are imprinting on young minds that see this modern day Boston Tea Party. Is it any wonder we continue to perpetuate hate, destruction and violence as a means of resolving our disputes? Is this really the example we want to set? We are better than this.

Maybe repatriation has to be more than just handing out cash to descendants dating back some 400 years, when clearly *some* good has come from descendants of slaves being here in the home of the free and the brave. You are bestowed with great opportunities as was demonstrated by the Johnson family dynasty. Chances are without slavery, you would not exist.

Your parents, parents, parents, parents, parents might likely have perished or taken up with another tribe thus altering the space time continuum. You were never born. So, perhaps instead of being the constant victim, you embrace a little goodwill, grace and gratitude that you ancestors suffered at the Master's hand so that you might live in riches. With a national debt closing in on $30T, maybe our imploding economy, our way of life, needs to be met with some restraint.

Maybe one way to serve up repatriations is to make all hard working middle class individuals earning less than $100,000 per year, gross income or wages, be excluded from paying any Federal or State income taxes. Furthermore, every black person from this day forward for the next 400 years is to be exempted from paying taxes on gifts, inheritance, property, sales or capital gains. This will definitely give generations of black lives the capital M in matter!

SHADOW PROGRAMS
Mentoring

While our country needs obvious direction, our youth need a new sense of direction as well. Many 'children' default to gangs for sheer survival, coercion or boredom. Others remain home behind locked doors as latch-key kids their faces down, glued to video games.

Kids need real leaders and genuine role models. Much like the Peace Corps of the sixties, we need leadership in the streets steeped in desire and commitment to execute our vision with innovative ideas.

One such program we ought to develop more fully is a "SHADOW" program where kids, from an early age, can experience all areas of endeavor such as where they might want to live, grow and effect change in the world.

Shadows will be afforded every opportunity to walk in the footprints of mentors casting their shadows. Envision this as a lifelong experience and relationship that will be paid forward for many generations.

SPORTSMANSHIP

<u>Under The Kodel Party
The President's Council on Fitness
would change its focus to
The President's Council on Sportsmanship</u>

We especially have to remove drugs and players as sports role models for millions of kids. We must promote exercise and nutrition, teamwork, integrity, self-control, anger, and above all, sportsmanship. We should encourage states to formulate role model programs in every community from the ground up.

We should increase the importance of how the game is played. The unfortunate reality is winning is tied to profits. Sports at the higher levels, is business, pure and simple. Cheating at your business is never justified. It is stealing--from the fans, the innocence of youth, your teammates, core values we hold dear and the athlete.

Cheating is as hollow as a victory gets. Kids watch college and pro sports and that behavior is emulated. We want to provide children with a more solid foundation of core ethics and the principles of sportsmanship.

When a Denver Bronco's football player (Peyton Manning's team-mate Aqib Talib) forcefully and with malice of forethought gouged at a lineman's eyes (Dwayne Allen) he should have had to turn in his uniform FOREVER! It was a blatant, purposeful, disrespectful display of the worst sort of sportsmanship ever. Moreover, this is Talib's default payback. It is appalling this is allowed by the league.

Talib walked right up to Allen after a play and jabbed his rigid index and middle fingers through the face guard right into the eye of a man, his opposing 'teammate.' He took a one game suspension and a little NFL pattycake fine and then had the audacity of entitlement nerve to seek an appeal. This is what's so ugly with professional sports—the bad player and the machine with no teeth.

Talib is a thug of the highest order. And it's NOT because he's black. It's because he is a criminal prick! No matter his athlete skills, his behavior is detrimental to the sport! A sport driven by greed, winning at any cost and rationalizing the malice act. No one takes responsibility. Had I been the coach, owner, general manager or commissioner, I would have not only kicked his ass off the team, but had him prosecuted for assault with the intent to purposely maim and blind player. Talk about a hostile workplace.

Shame on the team and ownership (John Elway) and rest, demonstrating a complete disregard for league leadership!

Children are watching!

Sportsmanship MUST BE honorable!

The very nature of competition is to have a clearly defined champion. Not every Olympic athlete earns a gold medal. Not every major leaguer hits 400. However, another truth, which lasts long after the game has ended, the whistle has blown, the bell has rung, or the last tock of the game clock ticks, is how you played the game or event. For this is what truly matters. Did you cheat, play or perform with honor, pride and integrity?

Over the last several years, the line has been blurred by coaches and players alike. Coaches tripping players; players faking injuries to stop the clock, also at the behest of the coach, so the lightening quick speed of an offense is slowed; players in the NFL have been seen stomping other players in the head and the groin, and so on. Steroid use in Major League Baseball is a national tragedy. (So is lying about it—under oath.) And yes, they are all truly sorry...(for being caught).

And don't get me started on the NHL. Brawling does NOT belong in any sport.

Winning at all costs is not the direction society wants. It is that very doctrine which betrays the game of "sport" which is carried forward in life.

As a society, we cannot function as a team if there are cheaters and liars amongst us; winning at all costs or cheating deserves no honor or respect. This is a social and a moral issue and not necessarily the business of government. We need your help to keep our kids healthy and enjoying their childhoods for as long as possible. Be conditioned, be trained, and execute as flawlessly as practical, and win or lose, hold your head high in either case, for you are a pure sportsman if you played hard giving your best effort, and you played with honor. Not only will your fans, coaches and communities respect you, you will respect yourself.

The End

Mike McCune – Bestselling Author

Big Deuce

(The Tom Dreyfus Novels): My Sweet Lorraine & Jake Leg

[Available on Amazon ~ FREE with Kindle Unlimited]

Set in Los Angeles in 1946, My Sweet Lorraine is a story of corruption, passion, loyalty, and of a homicide detectives' biggest mistake: [assuming]. Cynical veteran, Tom Dreyfus is called from vacation to do a favor for his boss: work what appears to be a routine investigation into the brutal murder of a beautiful young call girl. As Dreyfus and his partner, Munson, work scant evidence they uncover the woman was desperately trying to escape the sordid business, and that her clientele were some of the most powerful men in Los Angeles.

Mike often tells the story [and proves it with his yearbook] that he had a few classes in college with **Kevin Costner**. Kevin took one path and Mike the other. Both with dashing good looks, Mike became a prolific writer. This is his best detective gumshoe novella. It is an incredible period piece and a joy to read as the jargon of the day places you at the crime scene and throughout the investigation. You'll immerse yourself in the 1940's as Los Angeles police detectives track a serial killer.

DO NOT READ THIS BOOK IN THE DARK

OR ALONE!

These characters and dialogue that will stay in your head long after you've finished the book. Echoing Raymond Chandler, Elmore Leonard, Walter Mosley, and the Polanski-Towne film noir masterpiece, Chinatown, My Sweet Lorraine will go the distance & deliver a KO to the jaw. Better keep your guard up, because whatever happens is going to happen the hard way. ~ In 1949 the term 'serial killer' didn't exist; a psychopath just exhibited the same M.O.

Tom Dreyfus and his partner, Munson are back in Jake Leg and it's the hottest summer on record in Los Angeles. In this sequel to My Sweet Lorraine they investigate a series of four brutal murders of homeless men and women, seemingly anonymous faces on the streets that no one, especially the DA, cares about. Each of the victims was at one time a prominent member of society, and each had fallen from grace. Not one seems to have offered the least resistance to his killer. It's a race against time to find victim number five before the psycho, the self-proclaimed 'Angel of Mercy,' does.

LeGend M. Taliferro

January 30, 2016 - June 29, 2020

KANSAS CITY, Mo. — A 4-year-old boy was shot and killed inside an apartment near East 63rd Street and Paseo Boulevard during the early-morning hours Monday in Kansas City, Missouri.

KCPD officers were alerted around 2:30 a.m. to a shooting that took place at the Citadel Apartments in the 1600 block of Bushman Road.

Police said a toddler, who was identified Monday afternoon as 4-year-old LeGend M. Taliferro, was asleep in an apartment when he was struck by gunfire that came from outside the apartment.

LeGend was transported by private vehicle to an area hospital where he was pronounced dead.

Taliferro had a cardiac condition that required multiple open-heart surgeries. Having survived the surgeon's sword, a violent neighborhood bullet stole his young, innocent life.

Publisher's Footnote

The opinions expressed here are solely of the author and contributor and are not necessarily held by the publisher in whole or part.

Global proceeds from of this book and donations to go to America's inner city Boys and Girls clubs and as well as other foundations and organizations where education and tolerance programs are taught. At some point, we simply must turn the corner with our youth. Bigotry is a learned behavior with deadly consequences. We must not permit bigotry to exist. We must changes the behaviors and mindsets of adults and especially children from as early as day one!

Please Donate Today: PayPal.me/thekodelgroup

www.ingramcontent.com/pod-product-compliance
Lightning Source LLC
Chambersburg PA
CBHW061945070426
42450CB00007BA/1058